# BRIDAL GUIDE® MAGAZINE'S

## *How to Choose the*
## *Perfect Wedding Gown*

**DIANE FORDEN,** EDITOR IN CHIEF
WITH HEATHER MAC DONALD

D1104292

**WARNER BOOKS**

An AOL Time Warner Company

WARNER BOOKS EDITION

Copyright © 2004 by LifeTime Media, Inc. and Bridal Guide®
All rights reserved.

Bridal Guide® is a registered trademark of RFP, LLC and is used by permission

Warner Books, Inc., 1271 Avenue of the Americas, New York, NY 10020

Visit our Web site at www.twbookmark.com.

 An AOL Time Warner Company

A LifeTime Media Production
LifeTime Media Inc.
352 Seventh Avenue, 15th Floor
New York, NY 10001
Book Design and Line Illustrations: Amy V. Wilson
· Photos: Anne Barge; Campbell Design; Helen Morley; Ian Stuart;
Ines Di Santo; John Russell; Sincerity Bridal; Maggie Sottero;
Michelle Roth; Ulla-Maija; Watters & Watters; and Youlin.

Printed in the United States of America

First Paperback Printing: January 2004
10 9 8 7 6 5 4 3 2 1

ISBN: 0-446-67821-X
LCCN: 2003111162

Cover design by Claire Brown
Cover photo on left by Tim Rich
Center photo by Rhea Anna / Workbook Stock
Cover photo on right by San LaHoz

# Contents

# Foreword

*A*ll of us at *Bridal Guide* want you to enjoy the experience of finding the perfect wedding dress so that you look and feel beautiful on your wedding day. We know that you are about to embark on the most important shopping expedition of your life and that the gown you select will be the most meaningful—and probably the most expensive—garment you will ever own. In the following chapters, you will discover all you need to know to make the right purchase. We tell you when and where to shop, what styles are best suited for your body type, what your bridal party should wear, and much more. You will find expert advice on dress choices, design terminology, and accessory tips. We even provide charts and worksheets to keep your search on track, as well as timetables to help you stay scheduled and organized. After all, finding your dream dress should really be a heavenly experience. Have fun and enjoy the shopping—we know you *will* find the perfect dress!

Diane Forden
Editor in Chief, *Bridal Guide*

# BRIDAL GUIDE®
## MAGAZINE'S
### How to Choose the
# Perfect Wedding Gown

# *The Wedding Dress:*

## A Short History of a Long Gown

The wedding dress as we know it today, a full-length white or ivory gown, is a relatively recent convention. In fact, it didn't even exist until close to the mid-nineteenth century. Brides before that time weren't concerned with finding a new dress to wear on their wedding day, according to Shelly Foote, a specialist with the National Museum of American History, Smithsonian Institution, in Washington, D.C. A "Sunday best" dress, new or not, in just about any color (other than black) would do just fine for a wedding.

# *Hail, Victoria!*

Victorian dresses were quite ornate.

It wasn't until 1840, when Queen Victoria became the first royal bride to disregard the traditional silver or darkly colored brocade gown in favor of a full-length white lace dress, that the more familiar white wedding gown became popular. Newspapers throughout the world described her off-the-shoulder, full-skirted gown—and brides everywhere not only embraced this romantic new silhouette, but also chose the color white for their own wedding gowns. Victoria was also the first modern-day monarch to wear a wedding veil, which cascaded behind her so that her subjects could see her face. Eventually, veils became quite ornate, and by the 1870s they often enveloped the bride's body.

# Edwardian Elegance

In the early 1900s, the Edwardian style influenced bridal design and gowns like Eleanor Roosevelt's satin and lace gown, with its high neckline, long sleeves, and poufed shoulders, epitomized this new, more fitted silhouette. Dresses followed the contours of the body with full busts, cinched waists, and back bustles. Long lace veils or exquisitely embellished picture hats were favored.

The Edwardian "Look."

As the century progressed, a new ease in dressing influenced bridal style as well. By 1910, high necklines gave way to V necks and jewel necklines, and long, poufed sleeves disappeared in favor of flowing, inset sleeves. Expressing the graceful lines of the Art Nouveau movement, hemlines rose slightly to reveal shapely ankles and satin slippers, and softer, draped fabrics were frequently trimmed with lace and pearls. Headpieces ranged from floral-accented fabric caps with veils to wide-brimmed hats or simple headbands.

# The Jazz Age Twenties

The 1920s ushered in the age of the flapper, a modern woman who smoked in public, drank with the boys, danced until

A 1920s flapper bride.

dawn . . . and quickly tired of fussy dresses and layers of crinoline. These fringed flappers of the Roaring Twenties revolutionized the fashion scene and bridal styles followed suit. Simplicity ruled—no more ornate laces and beading. Silky fabrics, often in silk charmeuse or crepe de chine, skimmed the body in no-waist chemise styles that were banded at the hips and fell to just below the knee. Face-framing headbands complemented saucy bobs, and the cloche hat, a popular accessory for everyday wear, easily made the transition to wedding wear.

# The Hollywood Glamour Thirties

Depression-era audiences flocked in record numbers to the movies, and Hollywood was more than happy to accommodate their longing for glamour, beauty, and riches.

Film costume designers, like Dolly Tree and Irene may not be household names now, but the outfits they created, including wedding gowns for movie stars Jean Harlow, Carole Lombard, and Ginger Rogers, had an enormous impact on fashions of the day.

Hollywood stars' style reflected the sophistication and elegance of this Art Deco decade. On the big screen the dresses were shapely, decidedly more curvaceous than the boyish, linear silhouettes of the Twenties. The 1930s bride wore equally elegant ensembles and wed in satin, in a bias-cut gown that hugged the body in a sexy yet refined manner. These lean silhouettes were often closed at the side or buttoned down the back. Narrow sleeves extended to a point at the wrist and fishtail skirts with long trains glided across the floor. Attached to the back of her small pearled cap, worn back on her head, was a double-layered tulle veil whose fullness offered a contrast to the slim gown.

Simple lines characterized 1930s Hollywood style.
*"Florence" gown by Ulla-Maija*

# The War Bride Forties

War bride style reflected the country's serious mood.

Wartime . . . big bands . . . boogie-woogie bugle boys . . . Fashion in the 1940s pulled back from the overt sensuality of the previous decade. Materials needed in the war effort were restricted for commercial use by the government, including popular bridal fabrics like silk, which was needed for parachutes. As a result, synthetic materials, like rayon, were enthusiastically embraced for both everyday wear and wedding fashions. The classic Forties bridal gown reflected the more serious mood of the time. It had a fitted bodice, padded shoulders, and long sleeves that were slightly fuller on top. The waist was defined and skirts took on a gentle fullness. Lace was sometimes added around the neckline or at the end of long, fitted sleeves, but for the most part, the 1940s gown was more tailored and minimalist than wedding fashions in the past. Headpieces included snoods (netting decorated with pearls or flowers) or small crowns decorated with rhinestones and velvet flowers worn with veils to complement the popular page boy hairstyle.

# The Fabulous Fifties

The postwar, golden 1950s promised a decade of optimism. French designer Christian Dior created the "New Look"— a natural shoulder, cinched waist, defined bosom, very full skirt— that influenced brides everywhere.

Fashion celebrated femininity once again and H.R.H. Princess Grace of Monaco's wedding dress, with its form-fitting French lace bodice, cinched waistline, and full skirt, typified this ladylike feel. Gowns were more opulent, with lace and beading once again important decorative elements. Strapless bridal dresses also emerged, often paired with pretty satin or lace bolero jackets. And the crescent-shaped headpiece perfectly complemented a swept-back chignon or the era's signature short, curled hairstyle.

The 1950s offered brides a "new look."

# The Swinging Sixties

It wasn't long before American women found a new personality to lead them in fashion into the carefree 1960s: First Lady Jacqueline Kennedy. In outfits designed by Oleg Cassini, Mrs. Kennedy introduced the sleeveless sheath as a modern, formal look. Wedding designers followed suit and added a small cap sleeve to cover the shoulder. The flattering A-line dress, another Kennedy favorite, also became popular during the early Sixties for both everyday styles and wedding dresses. These A-line gowns often had empire waists and three-quarter-length sleeves, and head-pieces ran the gamut from the lacy mantilla to Juliet caps and satin pillbox hats. This was also the infamous decade of "rebellion," however, and fashion's more revolutionary styles like the miniskirt were favored by counter-culture brides. Others deemed themselves "hippie" brides and went barefoot, wearing long flowery dresses and real flowers in their hair at outdoor ceremonies.

1960s bridal styles were modern and carefree.

# The Back-to-Basics Seventies

Oh, happy day! After the turbulent 1960s, the 1970s bride turned to the nostalgic romanticism of the Victorian and Edwardian eras to define her style. One of the most memorable brides of this decade was Tricia Nixon, whose 1971 wedding to Edward Cox was televised from the White House Rose Garden. In a gown designed by Priscilla Kidder of Priscilla of Boston, Tricia wore a lace, princess-cut gown with a deep V neckline that emphasized fabric and fit. Made of white silk organdy and lace, the gown epitomized understated glamour with its fitted bodice and full A-line skirt.

Romance defined the 1970s.

As the Seventies progressed, wedding fashion became more romantic. High necks and full bishop sleeves were the rage. Gowns often featured a skirt ruffle twelve inches above the hemline, and more ruffles trimmed a lace bib on the bodice. In keeping with this decade's penchant for the fresh and natural, hair was worn long and loose, graced with a simple floral wreath and veil or a large picture hat.

# The Opulent Eighties

Beautiful beads and details defined the 1980s bridal gown.

Grand, opulent, over-the-top: the 1980s glorified excess and the quest for luxury dictated bridal styles. Television was a major influence on fashion as viewers tuned in to watch *Dynasty*, a soap opera saga of a wealthy Colorado family, featuring glitzy fashion by designer Nolan Miller. Bridal dresses soon began to look like elaborate white evening gowns dripping with sequins, crystals, and beads.

There is no doubt that the televised wedding of Princess Diana in 1981 set the standard for this decade's bridal styles. Her sumptuous ivory silk taffeta gown with its very full pouf sleeves, ruffled trim, billowing skirt, and theatrically elongated train enthralled a generation of brides. In the years that followed, gowns were lavishly embellished with lace, beading, bows, and ruffles. Shoulders and sleeves in large, poufed shapes emphasized basque-waist bodices, which were covered with pearled and sequined lace appliqués above heavily crinolined skirts with dramatic trains. The Eighties bride had arrived in all her splendor!

# The Minimalist Nineties

After the excess of the Eighties, women once more craved simplicity and elegance. The 1990s bride put the brakes on outlandish extravagance, opting for a return to sleek styles. Sleeves virtually disappeared as dare-to-bare dresses boasted the thinnest of straps or none at all. Strapless, halter, bateau, square-cut, and deep V necklines dominated. Embellishments were kept to a minimum, and gowns often had no lace or beading at all, opting instead for luxurious fabric and exquisite cut. Clean lines and simple styles emerged as A-lines, or sheaths, and these more refined ball gowns showcased a new sophistication that epitomized chic, modern style.

Simplicity is always in style.
*"Nadia Marie" dress by Maggie Sottero*

# Future Watch

Modern can take many directions.
*"Sorelle" dress by Ines Di Santo*

No doubt wedding-gown styles will continue to evolve as they reflect the fashion trends that lie ahead. New designers will thrill future generations of brides with their singular talent and creative flair. Unique use of fabrics, as yet unimagined, will help shape their vision into reality.

But no matter the styles, designers, or trends of the future, one thing is certain—the bridal gown will always be created to capture the beauty and joy of the woman who wears it.

*Chapter One*

# Doing Your Homework

Congratulations! You've got a diamond sparkling on your finger and are happily engaged. Now that you've said "yes," the excitement of planning your wedding is about to begin. And today, you can get started on one of the most thrilling tasks of all—searching for the wedding dress of your dreams. While you may have a certain style in mind, you'll want to shop around before you make a commitment because there is such a variety out there. After all, the gown you select will probably be the most meaningful (and expensive!) garment you will ever own. Your wedding dress not only has to be perfect—it has to be perfect for you.

When should you begin your search? If you're thinking "as soon as possible," you're pretty much right on target. You'll want to allow yourself at least nine months to find the ideal dress, order it, wait for it to come in, and have your alterations completed.

# *Time Crunch*

Already past the nine-month mark? Ask your bridal salon about rush delivery (which may cost an extra 10 to 20 percent) or buy a dress directly off the rack—more on that later.

## Budget Basics

Before you hit the stores, you'd be wise to create a budget, otherwise you may unwittingly find a "perfect" dress you simply can't afford, at least not without scrimping on other important aspects of your wedding attire. Remember, you can't walk down the aisle in sneakers—you'll have to purchase a pair of wedding shoes, and you may also want a headpiece, veil, gloves, jewelry, and a special handbag to match your gown. Lingerie is another consideration; you'll probably need special undergarments, such as a strapless bra or seamless panties to wear under your gown.

Wedding gown prices vary, starting as low as $200, although the average woman spends about $700 on her gown alone. But who says you're an average bride-to-be? Many engaged women spend significantly less or a lot more—either way, it's completely possible to have the look you want and stay within your budget at the same time.

Use our wedding-day attire budget worksheet to map out your expenses. We've included estimates for each item, but keep in mind they're not *all* required. You can cut costs painlessly by eliminating items you choose not to wear or purchase new, like jewelry or gloves.

# Wedding Day Attire Budget

| Item | Estimated cost | Your budget |
|------|----------------|-------------|
| Gown | $200 – sky's the limit! | _____ |
| Shoes | $40 – 300 | _____ |
| Veil/Headpiece | $100 – 300 | _____ |
| Gloves | $150 | _____ |
| Jewelry | | |
| Freshwater pearls | $40 – 250 | _____ |
| Cubic zirconia set in gold | $75 – 100 | _____ |
| Crystal and simulated pearls | $50 – 250 | _____ |
| Simulated pearls | $40 – 250 | _____ |
| Genuine pearls | $250 and up | _____ |
| Handbag | $20 – 150 | _____ |
| Bra | $36 – 75 | _____ |
| Crinoline/Slip | $30 – 100 | _____ |
| Hosiery | $8 – 17 | _____ |
| Garter | $12 – 20 | _____ |

# Cash or Credit?

As long as you've got the cash amount budgeted, it's preferable to pull out the plastic for any of these purchases. In fact, using a credit card will protect you against fraud, and if you use a card with rewards like frequent-flier miles, your gown purchase could also save you money on your honeymoon. If you purchase your dress at a department store, open a new store credit card and you may even get a discount on your dress.

But don't use the card to finance wedding dreams you really can't afford. Credit isn't free money, after all; it's a loan you'll have to pay back, along with interest and possibly other charges. End result: After your big day is over, if you can't cover the balance in full, you *and* your new husband could be saddled with major debt. Sure, limited funds may mean sacrificing that designer label, but imagine the satisfaction you'll feel when you find the perfect dress at a price you can comfortably afford—and believe us, it is out there.

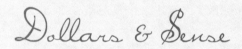

*Dollars & Sense*

- To save on your gown, browse bridal salon sale racks and consider bridesmaid dresses, too. Many are as elegant as wedding gowns, come in white or ivory—and cost much less.

- Search the regular dress department of any store for simple, unadorned white and ivory gowns. A seamstress can add pretty beading, lace, or other details to make it look special.

- You may not be able to sew your own gown, but if you're an artistic sort and handy with a needle, you may want to try creating your own jeweled crown, veil, or headpiece. Besides, the elements—tulle, combs or headband, fake pearls or crystals—are inexpensive enough to let you experiment.

- Designer showrooms in major cities often hold sample sales—a great place to find high-end designer dresses at discount prices. Call manufacturers or gown designers for the details on when and where these sales are being held.

- Buy "off-the-rack," a term that refers to purchasing the actual dress you try on in the store (rather than custom-ordering a gown). You can often save up to 50 percent off the price.

- Shop local consignment stores and online auctions, like eBay, for secondhand, worn-once gowns.

- A bridal salon's sample gowns may be available for sale at a discount. It can't hurt to ask.

# Getting Started

The best place to begin looking for a gown is . . . everywhere! As you search, keep a folder of styles and details you especially like— take notes, tear out photos from *Bridal Guide* and other magazines, and even draw sketches if they'll help you track your preferences. A few of our favorite places to find inspiration:

## Bridal Salons

Naturally, you'll want to get out there and hit the specialty shops, where you can see all of those gorgeous gowns up close and personal. Here you can sleuth out styles, feel fabrics, and try on any creation that strikes your fancy. Plus, you can get expert advice and opinions from the experienced sales staff.

# Time to Shop

*Whenever I drive by a bridal salon, the parking lot looks so packed, I don't even bother going in. How can I avoid the crowds?*

Naturally, weekdays—and even weekday evenings— are a safer bet than weekends, according to Elena Karafotias, buyer for Ultimate Bride in Chicago. "Everyone wants to come in on Saturdays," she says, "but some places are also open on Sundays, which is probably a less crowded day." If you can, take time off from work, and make appointments to visit several salons in one day. Or, try to schedule the first appointment of the day on a Saturday or Sunday, and beat the shoppers who prefer to sleep in on their weekends.

Certain times of year may be particularly hectic. Contrary to what you might think, the best months to shop are also the most popular wedding months: June, September, and October. Why? Brides who are about to be married have already found their dresses and had their fittings, explains Karafotias. On the other hand, June marks a big event for high school students, who shop at bridal salons during the months before the prom.

## Bridal Magazines

Your days of staring longingly at bridal magazines on the supermarket shelf are over—now those thick tomes are yours for the taking. As you thumb through, you'll notice they're chock-full of both editorial and ad pages of wedding gowns. See anything you like? Tear out those glossy full-color pages and file them away. (Be sure to record shopping guide information—usually found toward the back of the issue—before you toss the magazine.)

## Hollywood

The stars are known for their lavish weddings—complete with extravagant attire. While you may not want to spend a fortune on a one-time-only outfit, remember, you can probably find a similar but less expensive option. Check out today's celebrity picks in magazines like *People*, *In Style*, and *Us*. And get a close-up look at styles from yesteryear through today in films like *Father of the Bride* (1950 and 1991 versions), *Funny Face* (1957), *and My Best Friend's Wedding* (1997).

Hollywood glamour can be found in many styles.
*Gown by Anne Barge*

## On the Web

Wide awake at midnight thinking about your Big Day? Why not get online and check out wedding dresses? Like everyone else these days, gown designers have Web sites, too. Their addresses are usually listed in bridal magazines, either on the ad or in a directory in the back of the magazine. Start a list of designers you like, specific styles that appeal to you and retailers authorized to sell the gowns in your local area.

# Buddy System

**Q** *I'd like some input from my bridesmaids when I'm out looking for my gown, but I don't want to bring too many friends along. How should I choose my shopping pals?*

**A** Be extra selective, and narrow your pool of bridesmaids, relatives, and friends to just one or two who will accompany you on your excursions. Taking an entourage will only invite trouble—their hearts may be in the right place, but they're bound to offer conflicting advice and contradictory opinions, which can be confusing. And when you're searching for a garment as important and personal as your wedding gown, the last thing you need is added stress.

Start your search by shopping solo, so you won't be unduly influenced by others' opinions. Once you've had a chance to see what's out there, you'll have some ideas of your own about which looks appeal to you—and which do not. That's the time to get a second opinion from the friends and relatives you trust most (your mom and maid of honor, perhaps?). They can also help you keep track of the dresses and offer suggestions on a headpiece style and other accessories.

Worried that excluding someone may cause hurt feelings? Don't fret—most people you know won't expect to be included in your search for a wedding dress. If you choose, you can minimize the damage by delegating other planning projects or letting her help you select accessories, so she won't feel left out.

## Mom's Closet

Choose to wear your mother's gown and you'll inspire tears of joy—not to mention save tons of money and nail that "something borrowed" requirement while you're at it. Best scenario: her (now) retro dress is exactly your style. But if not, perhaps Mom can be talked into letting you have some alterations done, so you'll have a new look while wearing a gown that means something to both of you.

As you become more familiar with the thousands of styles to choose from, you may begin to notice a few common "threads" in the designs. Fact is, there are several popular wedding gown silhouettes, or shapes, you'll see again and again, like the traditional ball gown and the classic A-line. Use the proper bridal-style lingo in your notes (you *are* keeping track of the dresses you like most, right?) and you'll be able to describe exactly what you want on your next trip out. Use these illustrations to pinpoint the ones you like best.

### *Traditional Ball Gown*

You'll recognize this dress from your childhood dreams—it's the classic princess look with a dramatic full skirt and fitted, corset-style bodice. The waistline sits either at your natural waistline, slightly below your waist with a V shape in front or "dropped" at the top of your hips. It looks great on most brides, including full-figured women and those with an hourglass shape, but may not flatter the short-waisted.

*"Madison" gown by Maggie Sottero*

## *Classic A-Line*

Great for any figure, the A-line shape can provide balance for broad shoulders, lengthen a short waist, and camouflage wide hips. Fitted virtual panels extend in an A-line from the shoulders or bust to the hem, with no defined waistline.

*Gown by John Russell*

## *Sleek Sheath*

Slim and sexy, the sheath features a silhouette designed to hug your body—but not too tightly! Well-proportioned tall or petite brides, as well as full-figured brides, find that this style flatters their form.

*"Rose" gown by Ulla-Maija*

### Elegant Empire

Small on top?
Vertically challenged?
The empire style's
high waist and slim
skirt are perfect for
petite or bottom-
heavy brides, creating
the illusion of height,
skimming over a
midsection that
lacks definition
and defining a
modest bustline.

*Gown by Anne Barge*

### Sexy Mermaid

Calling all confident
brides! Even more
fitted than the sheath,
this hourglass shape
showcases every curve.
The flared hemline
at/or below the knee
looks like—you guessed
it—a mermaid's tail.

*"Gabor" gown by Maggie Sottero*

### Nontraditional

This category might include anything from a two-piece gown to a pantsuit to a tea-length or shorter gown. This kind of wedding attire is ideal for brides who are nontraditional themselves, in any sense of the word.

*Gown by John Russell*

### Vintage

You may choose to wear your mother's dress or even your grandmother's gown; but vintage styles are also sold in specialty shops. You can find authentic designs from the 1920s flapper girl through the 1970s dancing queen in such stores—and on the Web. Try eBay, or use

*"Larissa" gown by Ulla-Maija*

a search engine with keywords such as "vintage wedding dress" or "retro wedding gown" and see what turns up!

# Setting Your Style

Certainly you want to look your very best on your wedding day. And yes, you may even decide to indulge a childhood fantasy—say, playing the part of Cinderella with a full, flowing skirt and long train. Still, your wedding day look shouldn't stray *too* far from your everyday appearance. When you look back at your wedding photos, you'll want to see *you* in those snapshots, not some unrecognizable bride. Here, three style types to help you set your style.

## The Traditionalist

**Everyday wear:** Chic, classic clothing. Your neat, tailored, and feminine style works comfortably whether you're in a casual office setting or at a more formal after-hours outing.

**Shopping preference:** Department stores and high-end specialty retailers known for their professional wear.

**Bridal style:** If you're considering leaving the reception in a horse-drawn carriage, and you'd never dream of skipping the cake-cutting ritual, you're probably a true traditionalist who wants a fairy-tale wedding. You'll likely find yourself interested in a conventional white or ivory wedding gown. Try a strapless A-line, princess-style gown, or a dress with a full, ball-gown skirt.

## The Sophisticate

**Everyday wear:** Upscale designer clothing. The sophisticate looks for unexpected fabrics, striking color combos, and silhouettes that are sleek, clean, and modern. No one would ever accuse you of looking less than up-to-the-minute fashionable, but your look isn't just about labels—it's about projecting a polished and refined image for all the world to see.

**Shopping preference:** Department stores, specialty shops, designer showrooms, and designer outlets. You're not above checking out sale racks, either, if you can find this year's in-season items.

**Bridal style:** Do your plans include upscale elements like a harpist and string quartet during the ceremony or a jazz combo at the reception? A seriously sophisticated bride-to-be probably imagines a stylish, elegant affair for her wedding. Your dress should be equally chic and, like your wedding, not *too* over the top. Consider white or off-white with an emphasis on understated elegance rather than overdone details. Try a mermaid-style gown or a slim-fitting sheath in silk satin gazar.

## The Rebel

**Everyday wear:** All things trendy and offbeat. Clothes are your costume, and you choose what you wear for dramatic appeal. If it's unique and eye-catching, you buy it. And once an item goes out of style or becomes too mainstream, you move on to new territory.

**Shopping preference:** Vintage stores, thrift stores, specialty shops, and anyplace out of town—and thus out of reach of your pals at home.

**Bridal style:** You delight in the unexpected, and it follows that you're probably planning something exceptionally creative for

 your big day—the celebration might be a Halloween costume party or a destination wedding in a highly unusual location. Your style demands attire that reflects the same kind of creativity, so don't be afraid to try something different, like a vintage gown, pantsuit, or brightly colored dress. If you're not quite that daring, look for a wedding gown with distinctive details like an intermission-length skirt, pastel embroideries, or a blue sash that will set your dress apart.

## It's in the Details

Gorgeous gowns and stunning accessories often have one thing in common: little touches that scream *luxe*. When it comes to creating a standout look, the right balance of lavish details can make all the difference. Look for these outstanding trimmings on gowns, headpieces and hair accessories, handbags and shoes:

- Flirty feathers
- Faux fur
- Dazzling crystals
- Sparkling rhinestones
- Luxurious lace
- Funky fringe
- Brilliant beadwork
- Pretty pearls
- Elegant embroidery
- Ruffles or flounces

# Your Wedding Style

The wedding you envision, plan, and ultimately hold will undoubtedly have a style all its own—an important consideration before you start shopping for a gown. If you're having a formal wedding, for example, you'll likely feel most comfortable in a formal dress that reflects your motif. On the other hand, you don't have to restrict yourself *too* much. After all, as belle of the ball, you're entitled to stand out from the crowd! Yolanda Cellucci, owner of Yolanda's in Waltham, Massachusetts, offers these gown-selection guidelines to help you find a match for the three most common wedding styles.

## Formal

The Wedding: Black-tie attire, a sit-down dinner, and live music distinguish this type of affair. The setting is usually a reception hall in a lavish hotel. "It should have candelabras and special service," says Cellucci, "Men are in tuxes; women—from bridesmaids to guests—wear floor-length gowns."

The Gown: The bride's dress should be floor-length, not to mention elaborate and detailed. The color can be white, ivory, or an even brighter shade, as long as the style is formal evening wear. "While a cathedral-or chapel-length train isn't absolutely necessary, a long train would certainly be appropriate," Cellucci says. Gloves and a headpiece will also enhance the formality of your look.

## Informal

The Wedding: As destination weddings become more popular, so do weddings with an informal atmosphere. Given that the location may be a faraway beach or even your own backyard, guests may wear attire they feel comfortable in, like sundresses for women, or khakis and navy blazers for men. Dinner is buffet style; beverages might be as casual as B.Y.O.B. "It's usually more of a meet-and-greet than a sit-down affair," Cellucci says.

The Gown: Since an informal wedding is the least traditional wedding style, there are few guidelines for you to follow. Many brides opt for something unusual, like a vividly colored cocktail dress that can be worn again or an evening pantsuit in any hue.

## Semiformal

The Wedding: Somewhere between the formal and the informal is the semiformal affair. Usually held in a hotel, on a beach, or in a private home, this wedding can be a brunch, afternoon luncheon, or dinner, and depending on the time of day, women can wear short dresses, pantsuits, or cocktail dresses. The affair also features a buffet meal, but is pumped up a notch from the informal wedding with a band or a DJ. Men are dressed in tuxes or suits.

The Gown: Ankle-length, tea-length, and intermission-length gowns are considered semiformal; you could even opt for a wedding suit or go for a full-length, more formal gown. Again, any color is appropriate as long as the style matches the formality of your event. "The gown is usually more simple in design," explains Cellucci, and "the semiformal look does not call for a veil or headpiece."

# Ready, Set, Shop!

Searching for *the* dress will obviously require a bit more than a trip to the mall. Lucky for you, there are about 7,500 bridal shops,

# The "Second-Time" Bride

Since you're probably not interested in duplicating your first wedding—or marriage!—explore all the options that could set your second (or third or fourth...) gown apart from your first. If you've never worn the dress of your dreams, now is your chance. Or, you may find your fashion sense has changed, and you want a completely different look. In any case, choose a gown that makes you feel happy, comfortable, and beautiful.

## Culture Club

*Whether or not you choose to go traditional, you may want your wedding gown to celebrate your ethnic heritage. An Indian bride may want to wear a beautiful embroidered wrap in the style of a sari. A Chinese bride could incorporate the color red (which is considered lucky) into her attire by selecting a dress with red embroidery or beading. Research your heritage, and see what you come up with!*

# The Mature Bride

Thirty-something (or older) brides may believe they can't conform to conventional standards set for women marrying in their early twenties. But don't feel you have to forgo the veil or other elements of traditional wedding attire—they're appropriate for anyone who's young-at-heart, no matter what your age on your wedding day. If you feel a princess ball gown doesn't suit you at this stage, simply select another elegant bridal style, such as the sheath, mermaid, or A-line.

salons, and select department stores across the country, and they offer a nearly limitless selection.

Rather than visiting every shop and salon in town—who's got the time?—ask around for recommendations from friends who did their own gown shopping recently. Specifically, find out about the selection, the quality of the dresses, and the service at shops you're considering. Different salons have different atmospheres, from busy and bustling to more subdued, and you'll also find diverse personalities among the sales staff. Do your shopping in stores where you're likely to feel most comfortable—you'll be spending a lot of time there for fittings if you make a purchase.

## Have a "Dress Rehearsal"

Different hair and makeup styles work with specific gown styles, so think about your look when you go shopping. Up-dos and full makeup look best with formal gowns, and hair worn more naturally and simpler makeup better complement casual styles. Be sure to bring the proper lingerie, too—a strapless bra, seamless panties, and other support garments can be crucial when you're trying to look your best in a form-fitting wedding dress.

Once you've narrowed down your store options, make appointments before you head out, so you'll be guaranteed the individual attention sales staff can't always offer to walk-in clients. They'll be able to advise you about which gowns might suit you best while keeping you within your budget.

Remember, don't rush yourself. Even if the first dress you try on looks and feels like "The One," you should model several selections before making a final decision. A few shopping options:

## Full-Service Bridal Salons

Staffed by trained bridal consultants, bridal salons offer a wide selection (which could range from 50 to 200 dresses), including designer gowns, and many also carry bridesmaid dresses, accessories, and other items on your shopping list. You may be asked to register, which means filling out a few pages of general and wedding-related questions (names, addresses, wedding date, etc.) that help consultants identify your specific needs.

# Take Time Out

Saturday afternoon is a busy day at bridal salons. Be there when the stores open, or better yet, treat yourself to a weekday off from work and schedule several appointments—plus a relaxing lunch.

## Department Stores

You already know department stores are a great place to register for wedding gifts, but you should also be aware that many department stores have a full-service bridal salon right on site. While you can shop other areas of the store sans appointment, you'll need to call ahead before visiting the bridal salon. **Tip:** Department stores may carry fewer styles than regular salons—sometimes less than ten—but watch for "trunk shows," where bridal designers present their latest lines (check your local newspapers for upcoming events).

## Designer Boutiques

When you know what you want—a specific dress from a designer line—you may be able to go straight to the source by visiting the designer's retail boutique. There you'll be able to get answers to questions about style changes and alterations you may want done. If you adore the designer's line, but don't have a dress picked out, a salesperson can make suggestions. **Tip:** Schedule your appointment several weeks in advance, especially at the more exclusive boutiques.

## Discount Warehouses

Bargain shopping at these places can offer several advantages. For one thing, you're bound to save money. You'll also have the opportunity to try on dresses that fit right off the rack. That's because while most other bridal stores limit the sizes they keep on hand, discount warehouses stock dresses in several sizes. Plus, if you can try on a dress in your size, you can buy it—and perhaps avoid spending time and money on alterations. Some discount warehouses require an appointment and will do alterations for free or for a nominal fee if you make a purchase; in others you

# *Checking Up*

Scared by horror stories like *The Salon That Forgot to Order the Dress!* or *The Shop That Went Out of Business Overnight!*? Experts advise using the Better Business Bureau to conduct background checks before you shop. But remember that most retail stores in the country receive consumer complaints, including bridal shops. When checking records, don't evaluate just the number of complaints—look at the *nature* of complaints before crossing stores off your list. Word-of-mouth references are also good ways to assess a store's reputability—especially when your source had a recent experience with a particular retailer.

won't get much individualized attention and alterations are usually left up to you.

## Bridal Brokers

They're not authorized dealers, but they promise to deliver the same exact gown you tried on in a bridal store at a greatly reduced price. Sounds great, but beware: bridal brokers can't make any guarantees. Their orders may take a long time to come in, and in the end you could wind up with an inferior-quality knockoff. Dealing with bridal brokers can be risky financially, too. They require cash payment in full up front, and they don't take returns.

# Bridal Talk

Ready to speak bridal style? The world of wedding gowns has a language all its own. Here are terms you'll soon be tossing around like a pro.

### BODICE DETAILS

**Corset:** A period-style bodice that typically features boning sewn in for support and structure. Corsets are sometimes laced at the back or sides and are a good option for a bride seeking a "waist-cinching" effect.

**Shirring or ruching:** Fabric is tightly gathered and stitched into two or more parallel rows, resulting in a textural effect.

**Wrap:** Rather than a smooth front, a wrapped bodice features fabric that wraps around the body from the back or sides and is buttoned or tied in front. While some wraps replace fastening the bodice in back, most are purely for decoration. An asymmetrical wrap typically gathers to one side and is often sought after by brides seeking a slimming effect.

**Pleated:** Parallel folds of fabric that have been pressed and either stitched or steamed into place. Because pleats are typically horizontal, they're a good option for brides seeking to emphasize their upper body, but may not be an ideal choice for full-figured women.

## Dress Lengths

**Street:** Hemline falls just below the knee.

**Intermission:** Hemline falls to the mid-calf in front, floor-length in back.

**Tea:** Hemline falls to the lower part of the calf.

**Ballerina:** Hemline falls to just above the ankles.

**Floor:** Hemline falls ½ to 1½ inches from the floor.

## Laces

**Alençon:** Delicate floral or leaf design on a fine-net background, outlined with heavy threads to define the pattern and add more dimension.

**Battenberg:** Heavy lace made with patterns of linen braid and tape connected with decorative linen stitching.

**Chantilly:** Weblike floral pattern outlined with silk threads on a lace background (soft to the touch).

**Guipure:** Heavy lace designed to show large patterns over a coarse-mesh background.

**Lyón:** Intricate ornamental design delicately stitched onto a net background and outlined in silk or cotton.

**Point d'esprit:** Oval dots woven in a pattern on net fabric.

**Schiffli:** Intricate floral pattern embroidered directly onto the gown (similar to Alençon lace, but lighter).

**Venise:** Heavy floral or leaf pattern in needlepoint with motifs connected in lines.

## Necklines

**Bateau or boat:** Follows a straight line from shoulder to shoulder, covering the collarbone.

**Halter:** Fastens at the back of the neck, leaving the shoulders and back bare.

**Illusion:** A sheer panel or yoke made of tulle, net, organza, or lace that is attached to the bodice from just above the bust line to the neck.

**Jewel:** A rounded neckline that encircles the base of the neck.

**Portrait:** Wraps around the shoulder to "frame" the face; sits at the tip of the shoulders or just below to leave them bare.

**Queen Anne:** High-standing collar at the back of the neck that curves down to a sweetheart front.

**Sabrina:** Extends from shoulder to shoulder, curving slightly down below the collarbone.

**Scoop:** Rounded and low, dipping from the shoulders to just above the bustline.

**Square:** Shaped in a half-square or rectangle.

**Sweetheart:** Begins two inches inside the shoulder line, dipping to a heart shape at the bustline.

**Wedding-band collar:** High-necked, fitted, standing collar.

## SLEEVE STYLES

**Balloon:** Very large and poufed, extending from the shoulder to as far as the wrist.

**Bell:** Narrow at the top and flaring at the bottom edge into a bell shape.

**Bishop:** Softly gathered at the shoulders and full to the elbow, then fitted all the way down to the cuffs.

**Cap:** Very short and fitted, just covering the shoulder.

**Emma:** Similar to a cap, but shirred and slightly poufed.

**Fitted point:** Long with little or no fullness, falls to a point over the top of the hand.

**Gauntlet:** Detachable lace or fabric that covers the forearm and wrist.

**Gothic:** Extra-long and sheer, flows from the shoulders to well below the hands; split at the elbow for ease of movement.

**Juliet:** Long with a poufed top and fitted lower arm.

**Illusion:** Made of sheer, very fine net, often beaded, embroidered, or lace appliquéd.

**Leg-of-mutton:** Full and rounded from the shoulder to just above the elbow, tapering to a more fitted sleeve from the forearm to the wrist.

**Poet:** Fitted and narrow from the shoulder to the elbow, where it flares out.

**Pouf:** Short, full, and gathered; can be worn on or off the shoulder.

**Tulip:** Set in with overlapping fabric that curves into a petal-like shape.

## WAISTLINES

**Asymmetrical:** Begins at the natural waistline and angles down to one side.

**Basque:** A continuation of the bodice that falls below the natural waistline with pointed or rounded detail.

**Blouson:** Fabric is gathered just at or below the waist, creating a soft fullness.

**Dropped:** Falls below the natural waistline; may have points or rounded detail.

**Empire:** Begins just below the bustline.

## SKIRT DETAILS

**Bustle:** Fabric is gathered at the back waistline of the gown (may include the train).

**Flounce:** A wide piece of fabric or lace gathered and attached at the hem.

**High to low:** A rounded waistline that's inverted, so that the highest point rests at the center front of the waist, then gently curves down to the sides. Can be seen above a flat front or softly gathered skirt.

**Inverted basque:** An inverted-V waistline, in which the point rests at the center front of the waist, with straight lines extending diagonally from the center down to the sides. Because of the straight lines, an inverted basque is most often seen above a flat-front or inverted-pleat skirt.

**Natural:** A straight line that sits at your natural waist, or the smallest part of your waist just above your hips.

**Pannier:** Gathered fabric draped over the sides of the hips.

**Peplum:** Layered panels of fabric that fall from the waist to the hem in varying lengths.

**Tulip or petal skirt:** Overlapping skirt panels that resemble tulip petals.

**Tiered:** Layered panels of fabric that fall from the waist to the hem in varying lengths.

## Trains

**Sweep:** Short, barely sweeping the floor.

**Court:** Extends 1 yard from the back of the waist.

**Chapel:** Extends 1 1/3 yards from the back of the waist.

**Cathedral:** Extends 2 1/2 yards from the back of the waist.

**Extended or royal cathedral:** Extends 3 yards from the back of the waist.

**Watteau:** Attached to the shoulders of the gown.

# Dress Ideas

Gown by Michelle Roth

# Dress Ideas

_____

_____

_____

_____

_____

_____

_____

_____

_____

_____

_____

_____

_____

_____

_____

_____

_____

# Dress Ideas

# Sample Swatch Page

Attach fabric swatches here.

# Sample Swatch Page

Attach fabric swatches here.

*Chapter Two*

# Style Meets Form

Now that you've viewed several gowns—and probably identified a few personal favorites—you're ready to *really* get down to business. Choose wisely and you could find a dress that will naturally accentuate your positive points while minimizing areas that concern you. Sound too good to be true? Read on!

## Flatter Your Figure

When it comes to bridal gowns, some styles will suit you better than others, depending on your height, weight, and figure—though any dress you desire can be altered for your form. Here are a few of the most common body shapes and what styles best flatter each.

## The Triangle: *small bust, heavier at the hips*

**The goal:** Balance your proportions. Broaden your top half with full-sleeve treatments, padded shoulders, or pouf sleeves that extend your shoulder line. Add to your bustline with an off-the-shoulder neckline and intricate details, like a textured bodice accented with lace overlays, appliqués, and beadwork. De-emphasize your hips—and call attention to your waist—with an elongated bodice and a skirt with controlled fullness.

**Avoid:** Set-in sleeves, narrow shoulders, skirts with side panels or excess fullness, and body-hugging sheaths.

## The Inverted Triangle: *full on top, narrow at the hips*

**The goal:** Again, it's all about balancing proportions, this time by de-emphasizing your fuller upper body and playing up your bottom half. Minimize your shoulders, and add width to your lower body by choosing a gown with little shoulder details, simple sleeves, moderate padding, and natural shoulder lines. A simple bodice will downplay your bust and shoulders, while a full skirt or a style with skirt details such as pleating, peplums, bustles, sashes, and bows will bring attention downward.

**Avoid:** Full sleeves, empire waistlines, plunging necklines and slim, straight skirts.

## The Rectangle: *nearly equal bust and hips, minimal waist definition*

**The goal:** Add a few curves to your ruler-straight figure. Dresses with oversized shoulder and sleeve styles can add width to your top and shape to your overall appearance. A full, voluminous skirt, jewel or bateau neckline, and horizontal detailing create the illusion of curves by drawing the eye *across* the body (rather than just up and down).

**Avoid:** Slim silhouettes and soft, clingy fabrics.

## The Hourglass: *small waist, full hips and bust*

**The goal:** Make the most of your curves, while maintaining top-to-bottom balance. Try simple classic silhouettes, like sheaths and mermaid styles, but steer clear of too much detailing—otherwise you may create the illusion that you're heavier than you really are. Off-the-shoulder sleeves, V necklines, and strapless dresses are flattering options that let you flaunt your shoulders without upsetting the balance.

**Avoid:** Very full or ruffled skirts, pouf sleeves, highly detailed bodices, and high necklines that cover the shoulder area and minimize the bust.

## Petite: *under 5'4" and proportionally small all over*

**The goal:** Add height, and stretch your torso. Try a basque waistline, simple sleeves, modestly detailed shoulders, and vertical pleating. An A-line or princess silhouette is ideal; lengthen even further with a controlled-but-full skirt with minimal details. Sheath and mermaid styles complement slim petites.

**Avoid:** Voluminous gowns, especially in heavy satins, which will make a petite bride feel swallowed up.

## Full-figured: *proportionally heavy at hips, thighs, and bust*

**The goal:** Minimize hips and thighs, and create a smaller waistline. Draw the eye up with styling details around the neckline, and flatter a full bust in an off-the-shoulder portrait or **V** neckline with minimal detailing. A full skirt with fabric draping gracefully to the floor will camouflage lower-body concerns. A dropped **V** waistline will make your waist look smaller, and slenderize arms with long sleeves that taper toward the wrist.

**Avoid:** An overabundance of details, like beading, flounce, ruffles, feathers, and bows.

# Figure Fixers

Got a gripe about your appearance that you just can't overlook—
especially on your wedding day? Conceal your problem areas with
the right dress style and detailing.

**Problem:** thick waist
**Solution:** Minimize with an empire waistline.

**Problem:** short waist
**Solution:** Lengthen your torso with a princess-style dress.

**Problem:** long waist
**Solution:** Minimize in a style where the waistline is cut high
(such as a basque-waist gown).

**Problem:** heavy hips
**Solution:** Cover up in a full-but-controlled skirt without
bows, flounces, or ruffles (which would add more bulk to
your bottom half).

**Problem:** small bust
**Solution:** Maximize what you've got on top by accenting with
intricate details, like beadwork, embroidery, and sequins, and
opt for gowns with ruched, pleated, and ruffled details across
the bustline. Also, on-the-shoulder necklines work best.

# Figure Flatterers

Surely you're satisfied—even happy—with certain aspects of your
figure. Go ahead and show off the parts you're proud of, whether
you have shapely shoulders, long legs, or perfectly toned biceps.
Wedding gowns can play up all sorts of assets, such as a swanlike

# Sizing Up

 *I'm full-figured. What if the sample dresses in bridal salons aren't large enough for me to try on?*

Not to worry—some bridal salons specialize in plus sizes. Look under "Bridal" in the Yellow Pages, or ask other full-figured women you know for recommendations. Scan bridal magazines for plus-size dress ads, too; the ads often list phone numbers for stores where the dresses are sold. If you see a gown you like, call the stores listed in your area or call the dress manufacturer to track down the size you need in a shop nearby.

# Weight and See

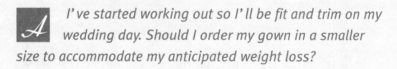 *I've started working out so I'll be fit and trim on my wedding day. Should I order my gown in a smaller size to accommodate my anticipated weight loss?*

Sounds like a smart idea . . . but no! Getting in shape is wise, no matter what motivates you. However, if you order a smaller gown, you'll be under major pressure to lose a certain amount of weight—and little can be done to make that small dress larger if you don't meet your goal. A better bet: order the gown in your current size and continue working out for fun, fitness, and the sense of satisfaction you feel. When the dress arrives, have it adjusted to your new size, whatever that turns out to be—during the fitting process.

neck or curvaceous legs. Think strapless, off-the-shoulder, mini-skirt, or intermission-length skirt, for example.

If you're leaning toward a gown that shows off a lot of skin, find out whether the venue for your ceremony has a dress code. Many religious sites do, and they'll sometimes restrict even the most tastefully designed dress. With a little creativity, however, you may be able to get around it. For instance, add a jacket, shawl, or scarf to your off-the-shoulder or strapless gown for the ceremony, then take it off for the reception.

# Color Concerns

Traditionally, as you surely know, the bride wears white, a color that has represented honor, innocence, and purity throughout history. But is white the right hue for you?

Before you decide, you should know that there are different *shades* of white—some may be better suited to your own coloring than others. According to Yolanda Cellucci of Yolanda's, women with dark hair often prefer the look of pure white, while those with blond, red, or frosted hair usually like ivory and "candlelight," a soft champagne shade that sets off their (often) porcelain skin tones. African-American women look great in ivory or white, while Asian brides and women with olive-toned skin usually opt for pure white, says Cellucci. Take a close look at your hair color and skin tone, and be sure to try on gowns in all shades of white to find the hue that is most flattering.

Unfortunately, store lighting often distorts color tones—and you certainly won't be marrying under fluorescent bulbs! Try to view dresses you like in more flattering, natural light, perhaps near a window. Also, know that sample dresses don't reflect a true color. White and other light-colored dresses simply can't hold on to their beautiful hue after hanging on racks and being tried on by many different customers. Ask your bridal retailer for a clean swatch that you can hold up to your face.

Keep in mind that the dress you try on can often be ordered in white, ivory, or champagne, and those aren't your only options. "People shouldn't lock themselves into only white or ivory," notes Steven Birnbaum, designer for New York City–based Birnbaum & Bullock. Pastel tones, like pink, peach, ice blue, and silver platinum, are gaining in popularity, and even bold hues of deep red or gold aren't unheard of these days. Another option: wear a white dress with colored details, like embroidery, lace, or beadwork.

## Tryouts

Of course, there's only one way to know whether you're going to like the color or style of a particular gown. You've got to try it on! Keep an open mind and try on a variety of gown styles. **Tip:** When you're browsing, don't limit yourself only to styles you love or dresses you believe will flatter your form—even those listed here. As long as your options are still open, keep an open mind. Leaning toward a simple dress? Consider at least one gown that's over-the-top ornate. Searching for an elaborately detailed dress? Take at least one subtly adorned gown into the dressing room with you. Many wedding dresses will look much better on you than they do hanging limply on the rack. You might be surprised to find yourself falling in love with a look you never even envisioned.

## Groom's Choice

Speaking of falling in love, you may want to consider your groom's good taste when selecting a gown. After all, *he* is the one you want to impress, right? In keeping with tradition, you probably won't want your husband-to-be to see the dress before the wedding, but that doesn't mean you can't suss out his opinion—without even hinting at your goal.

Start by considering the styles he likes. Does he notice when you wear certain outfits? Perhaps there's a pattern—he may tend to toss around the compliments each time you wear an off-the-shoulder shirt or a long flowing skirt. Next, consider what it is he loves about you—*besides* your sweet nature and quirky sense of humor. Does he happen to admire your slender waist and well-toned arms, for instance?

Dazzling your guy should be no problem now. Simply select a gown that incorporates the style elements you *know* he'll appreciate as you walk down the aisle.

# Comfort Zone

You're gazing in the dressing-room mirror, the gown is on, and—wow, you're gorgeous! But don't head to the cash register with your credit card just yet. Take time to imagine wearing this dress throughout your ceremony and reception. Move around a bit. Try sitting, hugging, and waving your arms around. You might even bust out a few dance moves.

Now, are the sleeves or shoulders binding? Is that extravagant beading a little weighty? Are the sequins on the bodice scratchy and irritating? If the gown feels slightly uncomfortable in the first five minutes you're wearing it, odds are it will be *extremely* uncomfortable after a few hours of dancing, dining, and mingling with guests.

With the wide variety of choices available, there's no reason you have to choose a dress with a skirt so long and full it presents a tripping hazard. Or a strapless gown that has you nervously checking your cleavage. Or even a silhouette that calls for a higher heel than you care to wear. Remember, you can be both beautiful and comfortable on your wedding day. All you need is a dress that makes you look good and feel good.

## In Season

Considering the time of year your wedding takes place can make a huge difference in how you feel on your big day. Case in point: Amy Shelley, of Saratoga, New York, who married in late July, just *had* to have her dream dress—a satin number with lace sleeves (yes, long sleeves) and a full skirt requiring a crinoline. While she loved the look of the gown, she now admits, "I was so hot, I almost passed out at the reception!"

Once upon a time, some fabrics were considered winter wear, while others were suitable for summer weddings only. Today, even though virtually all wedding gown fabrics and styles are seasonless, it does make sense to pay attention to tradition. Light fabrics (silk, chiffon, organza, gazar, and tulle) and summer styles (strapless, short-sleeved, or sleeveless dresses in silky, flowing fabrics) will naturally be more comfortable in warm weather. Weightier fabrics (duchesse satin) and winter styles (long sleeves and a full, crinolined skirt) are more logical choices when temperatures drop.

## Perfect Fit

Whether the gown you fall for is a perfect fit right off the rack or needs alterations, rest assured you'll have a custom-tailored look by the time your fittings are completed. Typically, it takes three fittings to get your gown ready, and you should take along the lingerie and shoes you plan to wear, so your proportions can be measured accurately.

When it comes time for your second or final dress fitting, bring along your mother or maid of honor, too. You might need some help getting into the gown before your ceremony or bustling your train during the reception, and you'll want her to learn beforehand how to do it right. Don't be shy—that's what attendants are for!

Also, speak up at your fittings if anything feels binding or uncomfortable. Remember all that jumping around you did when you tested your gown for comfort the first time you tried it on? Keep it up at the end of each fitting session. You'll want to make sure the end result is as comfy as possible.

# Gown Care 101

Once your dress is ready, should you take it home for storage in your closet or hang it on the back of your bedroom door? Definitely not. If you're like most brides, you'll feel most comfortable once the dress is safely in your possession—but think of the damage you could do. Rather than letting your gown get crushed or wrinkled before your big day, leave it at the shop until the week of your wedding. Bridal salons are equipped to store your dress properly, plus, it will be safely hidden from your husband-to be. When you *do* pick it up, keep it in its bag and hang it so that it's not leaning against any walls or doors (if you've got an indoor balcony, now's the time to use it). Unzip the bag slightly to let in some fresh air. On your wedding day, remove the gown from its bag and lay it across the bed on a clean sheet of cotton or plastic until you are ready to get dressed. Shut the door, and keep cats, small children, and other mess-makers away!

# At-Home Storage

*Q* *I've heard of bridal shops that burned down or went bankrupt and would prefer to take my gown home as soon as possible. How can I store it properly for a few months?*

*A* Anyone who's getting married is bound to be inundated with horror stories that end with a bride unable to obtain her already-paid-for wedding dress. Keep in mind that disaster certainly isn't an everyday occurrence, and if you've checked the shop out with friends and the Better Business Bureau, you're probably safe in assuming the store is reputable.

Still, you're not obligated to store your gown at the bridal shop. If you decide to keep your dress at home in the months before the wedding, just make sure you treat it right. Don't hang the dress for months on end (which could cause stretching) or store in direct sunlight (which could cause discoloration). Do lay the gown flat in a cool, dry room, stuff sleeves and bodice with tissue paper to prevent wrinkling, and cover for protection with a cotton sheet. About a week before your wedding, bring the dress to a professional dry cleaner or your bridal shop, so they can steam out any wrinkles.

# Finishing Touches

You didn't forget about accessories, did you? A complete bridal ensemble requires more than just the gown—even if you're going for an understated look. Select accessories to match your dress and wedding style (salespeople can help), and choose items that will complement your figure, height, and hairstyle.

## Headpiece

Opposites attract when it comes to your headpiece. Pair an ornate gown with a subtle pearl headband or a simple, clean-lined dress with a more elaborate jeweled tiara and veil. If you're having an informal wedding, think outside the box—top off your look with a hat, a garland of flowers, or a decorated comb. **Tip:** Before you make your final headpiece selection, consider the hairstyle you'll want. Tiaras or headbands work well with up or down hairstyles, bun wraps are perfect for tight chignons, and jeweled hair sticks offer lots of versatility.

## Veil

Taller brides can carry off a dramatic long veil, but a petite bride may want to scale down a bit. And if you've selected a gown with a beautiful back, why cover it up with a lengthy veil? If you do choose a long veil, remember, you have options. Feel free to change into a shorter veil (with assistance from your maid of honor) or detach it completely from your tiara for your reception. Also, like a headpiece, your veil should complement your dress as its opposite—a simple gown pairs nicely with a multilayered veil, for example. And decide how you want to wear your hair prior to making a decision about a veil.

## Jewelry

When it comes to wedding day jewelry, less is usually more. Strip your fingers of everyday rings and leave your everyday watch at home—you don't want any other trinkets to compete with your engagement ring and new wedding band.

If your dress has an open neckline that cries out for a necklace, top choices include a traditional pearl choker or strand, or a pearl or diamond pendant. Why are these items so popular? They offer understated elegance, whether you wear fine or costume pieces. Small pearl or diamond stud earrings are other favorites.

Keeping it simple doesn't mean you can't be stylish. If you're wearing subtle, crystal hairsticks and no necklace, dangling "statement" earrings are appropriate. You *can* opt for more ornate jewelry if you're wearing an understated gown. Search out unique pieces in bridal salons, vintage shops, jewelry stores, and in the jewelry boxes of female friends and relatives (something borrowed)—with permission, of course!

## Gloves

A pair of gloves can provide an easy-but-elegant accent to any sleeveless, strapless, or short-sleeved wedding gown—obviously, not if your dress has long sleeves! Match the length of your gloves to the size of your sleeve: wrist-length gloves go with just about any short-sleeve style. Try opera-length (over the elbow) with sleeveless or strapless dresses, and gloves that come to just below the elbow with short- or cap-sleeve gowns. Just be sure the top of the glove doesn't meet the bottom of your sleeve; allow a few inches of skin to show in between.

One caveat: if you decide to wear gloves, make sure you can remove them easily—without using your teeth! While you'll want to wear them down the aisle, you should shed them at the altar so your fiancé can place your ring on your finger. Hand them, along with your bouquet, to your maid of honor to hold. After the recessional, you can put your gloves back on—you'll want to wear them as you enter the reception and during special dances (your first dance as a couple, your dance with dad). From then on, you can either wear your gloves a while longer—because you just love the look!—or take them off.

## Essentials

Gloves, jewelry, a veil, and a headpiece are always optional, but there are other items every bride needs and can't go without—shoes and lingerie. In selecting both, comfort is key.

## Shoes

On your wedding day, you'll take one of the most significant walks of your life—that heart-pounding, joyful stroll down the aisle. So be sure to dress those tootsies in comfort and style. Best bets: don't go higher than a $2\frac{1}{2}$-inch heel (no stilettos, please!), and consider a shoe with a wide toe box or open toe to avoid friction and pressure when you hit the dance floor. Make certain you get a good fit (not too tight, not so loose they're slipping off). You should break in shoes before your wedding by wearing them around the house—with stockings, so you won't get blisters.

As for style, your options are plentiful—sexy, strappy sandals, slides, pumps, slingbacks, and mules. Naturally, they should match the style of your gown and suit the season as well. Now's your chance to buy shoes in a dressy fabric, such as satin, peau de soie, or silk shantung (workaday leather just won't do). And if the shoes you choose are accented with colorful embroidery, lace, pearls, or crystals, these details can mirror the design of your dress. Pair ornate shoes with a simple ensemble, and sleek, unadorned shoes with an elaborate dress.

## Lingerie

Don't let granny panties and a sports bra spoil your look today, ladies. Invest in top-quality foundation garments that can: 1) provide support where you need it; 2) create a clean, smooth line under your dress; and 3) make you feel extra-special and sexy!

The ensemble underneath your gown could include any number of items—a long-line, strapless bra, a body-slimming slip, or seamless panties among them. Unsure about what your gown and figure require? Ask sales staff at the salon where you purchase your dress (many bridal salons also sell appropriate and specialty lingerie), or visit a specialty lingerie shop or the lingerie section of a department store. Don't leave lingerie shopping to the last minute. Some undergarments may need to be custom-fitted, and you'll want to wear them to your dress fittings to ensure a proper fit.

## Detail Decisions

 *How should I decide whether I need gloves, jewelry, and other bridal accessories?*

Take some time to consider the style of the gown you've selected and, once again, the look you want. Ornate embellishments can give a simple dress a more formal appearance; understated accessories will subtly complement a lavishly detailed gown. Look for ideas that appeal to you in all the places where you started searching for your dress — bridal magazines, bridal shops, department stores, etc.

You can also get professional opinions from the sales staff who sold you your dress. They'll advise you about which accessories will look best with your bridal attire; the shop may even have many of these items on hand. But don't feel pressured to make any spur-of-the-moment decisions. Accessories don't have to be bought when you order your dress — you can wait until a few months closer to your wedding to make those purchases.

# *Emergency Kit*

Spilled wine? Who cares! Torn pantyhose? No problem! If you're prepared, that is. Pack an emergency kit, place it in your mother's or maid of honor's care, and put worries out of your mind. Top twenty items to head off disaster:

- ❑ Thread to match your gown
- ❑ Thread to match bridesmaids' gowns
- ❑ Sewing needles
- ❑ Safety pins
- ❑ Scissors
- ❑ Nail polish to match the color you're wearing
- ❑ Clear nail polish for hosiery runs
- ❑ Extra hosiery
- ❑ Spot remover
- ❑ Nail glue
- ❑ Band-Aids®
- ❑ Aspirin
- ❑ Mouthwash
- ❑ Clear solid antiperspirant (for underarms, palms of hands, soles of feet, and anywhere else you sweat)
- ❑ Foot powder
- ❑ Face blotting papers
- ❑ Bobby pins
- ❑ Hairspray
- ❑ Tissues
- ❑ Makeup

# Style Specifics

When you start shopping for accessories, you may be surprised to learn how many different styles of veils and headpieces are available. Here, a glossary of terms and definitions.

### VEILS

**Ballet or waltz length:** Falls to the ankles.

**Birdcage:** Stiff, wide-mesh veil pinned to the crown of the head, covering the face and ears to just below the chin.

**Blusher:** A short, single veil worn over a longer veil; covers the bride's face as she enters the ceremony and is lifted back afterward.

Cascade: Several layers of veiling in varying lengths; after the ceremony, the longer layers can be removed leaving a short, full veil.

Cathedral length: Falls $3\frac{1}{2}$ yards from the headpiece; usually worn with a cathedral train.

Chapel length: Falls $2\frac{1}{2}$ yards from the headpiece.

Fingertip length: Touches the fingertips when the arms are held straight at the sides.

Flyaway: Multiple layers that brush the shoulders, usually worn with an informal dress.

Mantilla: Lace-trimmed veiling that frames the face; can be worn on its own or placed over or under a tiara.

Pouf: Short, gathered veiling attached to a headpiece; usually worn with an informal dress.

## HEADPIECES

Half hat: A small hat covering half or less of the crown of the head.

Halo: A fabric-and-wire band that circles the forehead and is decorated with pearls, sequins, or flowers.

Hairpins

Hairpins or hair sticks: Jeweled hair ornaments that can be sprinkled throughout the hair.

Juliet cap: A small cap that hugs the back of the head.

Juliet cap with pouf veil

Picture Hat

Snood

Tiara

**Picture hat:** A wide-brimmed hat decorated with lace, pearls, or sequins.

**Pillbox:** A round, structured, brimless hat worn on the top of the head.

**Profile:** A floral comb worn asymmetrically on one side of the head and adorned with lace, pearls, or crystals.

**Snood:** Netting decorated with pearls, sequins, or flowers worn at the nape of the neck to cover hair worn in a chignon.

**Tiara:** An ornamental crown of pearls, crystals, rhinestones, or lace worn on top of the head.

**Wreath:** A circle of flowers that sits above the crown of the head or lower, encircling the forehead.

# Notes

# Notes

# Notes

# Notes

*Chapter Three*

# Pulling It All Together

As the search for your wedding gown gets more serious, keep decisions you've already made in mind. After all, you've identified your personal style, figure type, and wedding style. You've set boundaries in terms of budget. Pretty soon, you'll be ready to stop shopping and make a final dress decision. You can't plan forever—your wedding day is fast approaching!

## Wedding Gown Countdown

Start early—meaning at least nine months' worth of shopping days before your wedding—and you'll have no trouble pulling together a beautiful bridal ensemble.

### Six to nine months:

❑ Begin shopping for the dress of your dreams.

❑ Narrow down options, make a decision, and order your gown. Be prepared to part with a down payment of 50 percent of the cost of the dress, and get the lowdown on alteration fees, the shop's cancellation policy, any free services, and the date your balance is due. Also, confirm your dress delivery date, and ask about the fittings policy: how many you'll need to attend, what to bring, how long each session will last.

### Six months:

❑ Shop for bridal accessories (shoes, lingerie, jewelry, etc.).

### Three to six months:

❑ Order your headpiece, wedding shoes, and other accessories. Your dress should arrive three to four months after the order is placed. Attend your first gown fitting. (If your shoes aren't in yet, bring along a heel that's similar in height.)

### One month:

❑ Attend your second fitting. Bring your headpiece, and this time make sure you've got your wedding shoes with you.

### Two weeks:

❑ Attend your final fitting. Bring along your mother or maid of honor if you need someone to learn how to bustle your dress and secure your headpiece. Raise your arms, hold them straight in front of you: The dress should feel comfortable without any pulling or stretching of the fabric.

### One week:

❑ Bring home your wedding dress! Pick it up as close to your wedding day as possible, so it won't get wrinkled in storage at your house. Leave it in its bag, unzipped slightly to prevent moisture, and hang it so it isn't leaning against walls or doors, such as over a balcony or off the handrail to a staircase. On your wedding day, take the dress out of the bag and lay it on a clean white sheet on your bed until you are ready to get dressed.

# Size Surprise

Once you're ready to place an order, your bridal consultant will measure you and recommend a size based on the size chart for your dress. Bust, waist, and hip measurements are standard; other common measurements include back shoulder width (from shoulder blade to shoulder blade), center back (from the base of your neck to your natural waistline), inside sleeve length (from armpit to wrist), arm girth (around the upper arm), waist to hem (from your natural waistline to the planned hemline), and low hip (which falls 7 inches below your natural waistline).

Don't be shocked when you learn your measurements translate to a much larger size than you'd anticipated. Size charts for bridal attire are different from the measurements used for everyday clothing—as in, wedding gowns run smaller than casual dresses. In addition, sizes also vary from designer to designer.

What to do if your consultant recommends a size larger than the sample gown you tried on—which fits perfectly? Remain calm, and rest assured she knows what she's doing. Sample gowns are tried on so many times they've stretched, meaning a size 10 dress might comfortably fit a size 12 or even a size 14 body. But as long as you order the right size for your figure, who cares? Remember, size is just a number.

## Bring in the Pros

For a small fee, many brides hire the fitter to help them dress before the ceremony and bustle the train for the reception. If you're interested, ask about this service by your second fitting, at least one month in advance of your wedding. That way, you'll have plenty of time to find someone else if your fitter is unavailable. Ask the salon or recently married friends for recommendations.

# Alterations

Ready for another surprise? Despite your consultant's careful measurements and diligent use of the designer's size chart, your gown *won't* fit perfectly when it arrives. The goal in ordering a specific size is simply to get the closest fit possible, ensuring you won't be stuck with the expense and bother of having a size 12 cut down to a size 8, for example. Nerves and other pre-wedding jitters may also cause your weight to fluctuate, and even a loss of a few pounds may affect the fit of your dress—sometimes up to the last minute. At the very least, you'll most likely need the hem shortened, bodice side seams taken in, and sleeves and shoulders adjusted. If your gown has a train, you may also want a customized bustle made to gather it up for the reception.

Intricate beadwork, delicate lace, and other details make altering a wedding gown a job for pros only, so many bridal salons offer alteration services with an in-house seamstress, who is paid a regular salary by the shop. According to Bernadette Pleasant, owner of Bridal Suite of Manhattan in New York City, customers may be charged "a la carte," for hemline, waistline, and other work, or the shop might charge a flat fee for alterations. If any of the alterations go "above and beyond," such as an extra-complicated hemline, an additional 25 percent fee isn't unusual.

Shops that don't employ a seamstress of their own may refer you to an independent contractor of their choice or offer you a selection of outside resources. In any case, if you have a seamstress in mind—someone with gown experience and a proven track record of success—consider enlisting her services. There might be some stores that won't object, since some retailers don't earn an additional profit even when you use their in-house seamstress. But find out what your salon does and does not provide in terms of in-house services before you call upon outside help.

Speaking of which, you're probably wondering just how much these alterations are going to cost you. The truth is, costs vary greatly depending on the work you need done. And even something simple like shortening a hem can be pretty pricey when you're talking about a wedding gown. For example, a dress with lace trim at the hem will need to be shortened at the waistline rather than the hemline, making it a much more complicated—and expensive—job. Since prices do vary, you might pay anywhere from $200 to $1,000 for certain alterations, says Pleasant.

Whatever the expense, you can take control of the situation early on. Obtain a written estimate when you purchase your gown or go for your first fitting. If you're asked to put down a deposit on alterations, do so with a credit card for your own protection. And have fun tracking the progress of your alterations. Most gowns require three fittings, so you'll be able to make sure the changes match your expectations.

# Off-the-Rack or Custom-Ordered?

Yes, you have a choice! Simply defined, "off-the-rack" refers to the dresses you find at your fingertips in a bridal salon. While you won't likely purchase the *actual* sample gown you try on (unless you shop at a discount warehouse), the store's bridal consultant will order the same exact dress in the size and color you need. This gown won't match your measurements perfectly, but you will get a better fit than the sample, and alterations can take care of the rest.

A "custom-ordered" gown, on the other hand, is your opportunity to create the dress of your dreams from among the designs on the rack—and beyond. It's your chance to "customize" a dress so it suits your needs, explains Pleasant. "A custom order is where you really make the dress work for you," she says.

For example, religious, conservative brides may want a gown with long sleeves—then they fall in love with a sleeveless dress. A custom order can include adding sleeves, building up a neckline, even combining the top of one beloved gown with the bottom of another. Custom orders offer options beyond size and color, giving you the chance to play dress designer and order exactly what you want.

Costs for custom orders can still stay low, according to Pleasant. It all depends on the work you need done. Each change will carry a fee, which should be indicated on your contract with the store. Also, these changes, like the gown itself, usually require a 50 percent deposit when your order is placed.

# Made for You

It's the perfect gown, you've got a picture from a magazine, and it costs, well, way more than you could ever afford. Don't lose hope—a professional seamstress might be able to make the dress for you, at a much lower price.

When you hire a dressmaker, you buy the pattern (or present a picture), as well as fabric and details, like lace and beading. If you're looking to save money, you can start by making smart purchases here. You'll also pay for labor, so the simpler the pattern, the more likely you are to beat retail price tags. On the other hand, an elaborate design could cost far more than a dress from a shop. According to Pleasant, prices to have a gown hand-sewn start as high as $1,000 for even the most basic styles—and the cost can go even higher depending on the beadwork and other details you've selected.

If you want to have a dress made, be sure to choose a true professional—someone with experience in wedding gowns. Ask around for references before you meet with a dressmaker or, if you find someone on your own, request the phone numbers of previous customers. Once you've decided on a seamstress, be sure to communicate regularly with her about the dress you want and the final results you can expect.

# Saved!

Got your heart set on wearing your mother's wedding dress or a secondhand gown you found in a consignment shop or vintage store? Check it over carefully for signs of damage—stains, torn lace, missing beads, yellowed fabric, ripped seams, etc. A gown that's been worn before often needs some work before it will be suitable for another trip down the aisle. In many instances, only a professional can tell you whether repairs are possible and how much they'll cost you. Get an expert opinion from a service like Imperial Gown Restoration Company, in Fairfax, Virginia (www.gown.com), which cleans and restores vintage wedding gowns with the same special techniques used by museums and conservators.

If you spot any stains, try to determine what might have caused them (white wine turns brown with age, covered metal buttons can leave rust marks), so you'll be prepared for a discussion with your dry cleaner. When it comes to rips and tears, a seamstress should be able to help. Bring the dress along if you already own it, or just drop by with questions before making a purchase.

Severe damage—like a tear down the front of the skirt—can't always be undone, but there may still be a way to make the dress wearable. Perhaps your seamstress will recommend covering the tear with lacework, or even replacing the entire skirt. Major alterations can be costly, but they could be worth the expense if your heart is set on a particular dress.

Alterations can also transform a vintage gown that hasn't suffered damage, but isn't quite right for your modern-day wedding. Case in point: Katie Bloom, of Portland, Maine, planned to wear her mother's dress on her wedding day—and it hadn't been cleaned in more than thirty years. Though it turned out the gown wasn't stained or damaged, it did have one major flaw: the sleeves. They had been perfect for her mom's February wedding but were not so ideal for Bloom's August nuptials. Solution: Katie had the sleeves removed and transformed a winter dress into a summer style.

# Wedding Gown Worksheet

The shop where you purchase your dress should have this information on hand, but you can keep track of the details, too, so you don't forget the cost or miss your fittings. The more organized you are, the less you'll have to worry about!

Description: _____

Designer: _____

Size: _____

Price: _____

Contact: _____

Address: _____

Phone:_____

Alterations charge:_____

Payment policies:_____

First fitting date: _____

Second fitting date:_____

Final fitting date: _____

Estimated delivery date:_____

# Satisfaction Guaranteed

When it comes down to placing your order and making your—often hefty—50 percent down payment, buying a bridal gown will feel like serious business. Treat it as such by protecting yourself against problems, whether caused by innocent miscommunications or premeditated fraud. Get everything you can in writing, and you'll know exactly what you're getting and when. Don't let the salesperson swipe your credit card till you've read over your contract and feel comfortable that you understand and agree with all terms and conditions. The contract should include:

- Price and payment schedule

- A description of your dress, including the style number, manufacturer, color, and size ordered

- Any changes you want made to the design

- Extra charges (for shipping, custom design, etc.)

- An estimate for alterations

- Store refund policy

- Store responsibilities for errors made by the manufacturer, during shipping or during alterations

- Any discounts or extra services

- Anticipated delivery date

- Confirmation number

- Store policy on fulfillment of tailoring obligations (after three fittings, when you're satisfied with the fit, etc.)

# Who's Buying?

Tradition holds that the bride's family pays for her wedding attire. But there are plenty of reasons why you might want to make the purchase on your own—perhaps you're an established career woman, or you suspect relatives will use the power of the purse to decide the style of the gown and accessories you should choose. In any case, this rule can be bent a bit, even if you can't afford the entire expense yourself. Today's bride-to-be often splits the costs with her fiancé or her parents.

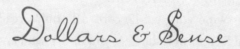

*Dollars & Sense*

- If you don't have a credit card to use to purchase your dress, write a check, so you'll have a record of the payment.

- Be aware that the deposit on your dress is usually nonrefundable.

## Dress for Success

Think you can just hop into your gown and be on your way? Guess again! Before you even touch that dress, your hair should be done and makeup applied. Paint your nails (or get a manicure) the day before the ceremony, so they'll have plenty of time to dry without smudging.

When you're ready to get dressed, wash your hands—just in case your fingers are smeared with makeup—and allow at least an hour and a half to put on your undergarments and gown. Once you're dressed, put on *all* accessories. (If you leave anything till the last minute, you just might forget it altogether.) Secure your headpiece last—unless the stylist put it in place when you had your hair done—and you're ready to walk down the aisle!

# *Important People & Places*

Name _____

Address _____

_____

Home Phone _____

Cell Phone _____

E-Mail _____


Name _____

Address _____

_____

Home Phone _____

Cell Phone _____

E-Mail _____


Name _____

Address _____

_____

Home Phone _____

Cell Phone _____

E-Mail _____


Name _____

Address _____

_____

Home Phone _____

Cell Phone _____

E-Mail _____

Name _____

Address _____

_____

Home Phone _____

Cell Phone _____

E-Mail _____


Name _____

Address _____

_____

Home Phone _____

Cell Phone _____

E-Mail _____


Name _____

Address _____

_____

Home Phone _____

Cell Phone _____

E-Mail _____


Name _____

Address _____

_____

Home Phone _____

Cell Phone _____

E-Mail _____

Name _____

Address _____

_____

Home Phone _____

Cell Phone _____

E-Mail _____


Name _____

Address _____

_____

Home Phone _____

Cell Phone _____

E-Mail _____


Name _____

Address _____

_____

Home Phone _____

Cell Phone _____

E-Mail _____


Name _____

Address _____

_____

Home Phone _____

Cell Phone _____

E-Mail _____

Name _____

Address _____

_____

Home Phone _____

Cell Phone _____

E-Mail _____


Name _____

Address _____

_____

Home Phone _____

Cell Phone _____

E-Mail _____


Name _____

Address _____

_____

Home Phone _____

Cell Phone _____

E-Mail _____


Name _____

Address _____

_____

Home Phone _____

Cell Phone _____

E-Mail _____

*Chapter Four*

# Gown Alternatives

A traditional white or ivory gown is not every bride's idea of the perfect wedding look. And these days, that's just fine.

"It's a very exciting time for bridal. Just ten years ago, wedding dresses had a uniform look," says Laurie Brookins, fashion editor at *Bridal Guide* magazine. "Now there's such a variety of designs available brides should feel free to look for a gown that ultimately reflects their personal style."

So if you're a third-time bride and "nontraditional" is your everyday look, but you have your heart set on wearing a formal white gown, go for it! If, however, you plan to wear alternative wedding attire, get ready to explore your many options.

## Wedding Suits

A jacket-and-skirt ensemble that's appropriate for a wedding is nothing like a business suit. Instead, it's made in luxurious fabrics

that are perfect for evening or for a formal and sophisticated afternoon wedding. Fabrics such as silk crepe, silk shantung or satin, or silk Fortuny, with such details as beading or embroidery will give a wedding suit an elegant feel. Where to buy? Specialty boutiques and high-end department stores stock wedding suits, especially during holiday seasons. Or, you can have one made. A good dressmaker will likely have many ideas for wedding outfits and can work with you to come up with a two-piece look that is completely your own—and as exquisite as a traditional gown.

## *Golden Rule*

There's only one "rule" every bride should be sure to follow when selecting wedding-day attire, according to Laurie Brookins: "You need to be respectful of religious criteria." Many churches and other houses of worship require shoulders to be covered. That doesn't mean strapless and spaghetti-strap gowns are out, however. Most designers are aware of this restriction and offer stoles, shrugs, and other coverings that can be worn during the ceremony and removed afterward for a bare-shouldered, sexy look at the reception.

# Vintage Gowns

Before you start shopping, ask yourself: Do I want a genuine vintage gown or a vintage-*style* dress? That way you'll know whether you need to do the extra legwork required to find an authentic antique. If the real deal is what you're after, shop online auctions, consignment stores, and family members' attics (with permission, of course) for a hand-me-down gown, keeping in mind that the further back in history you go, the more difficult the challenge. For example, you may have a hard time

A vintage feeling can be achieved with a new dress.
*"Alva" gown by Ulla-Maija*

finding a Victorian-era dress to fit, since gowns—and people —were much smaller back then.

On the other hand, if you're willing to forgo true vintage, you should still be able to find the dress you're looking for among today's styles. Designers often reference all eras in their designs, from the 1920s (when flapper fashions featured scalloped and handkerchief hemlines) to the 1950s (when boxy jackets and slim skirts were in) to the 1970s (when empire waists and leg-of-mutton sleeves updated Victorian and Edwardian dresses). If you have your heart set on a certain look, you can find a similar style from a current designer today.

# Getting It Right

**Q** *I know how I want to look on my wedding day but can't seem to find a store that stocks the exact gown I have in mind. Sometimes the fabric is wrong or there's something I don't like about the style. Help!*

**A** Don't be afraid to ask for what you want—even when you don't see it anywhere in the store. If color is the issue, most dresses come in both white and ivory, and may be available in other hues, too. Styles can be altered as well. If you find a lovely spaghetti-strap gown that would be perfect with sleeves, for example, many designers will add them. They can also add a "modesty panel" to a dress that's too low-cut for your comfort. If you see a gown you like but would prefer it in a different fabric, that may also be possible with a special order.

Even if nothing on the racks resembles your dream dress, don't give up hope. Bridal shop owners visit designer shows and see lots of styles they may not have purchased for their salons. If you describe what you're looking for, the store owner might recall a designer who makes that gown and will most likely be happy to special-order it for you. Still can't find the dress you're after? Consider having a seamstress create the original design you have in mind.

## Destination-Wedding Gowns

If you're planning a wedding away from home, you'll want to give some extra consideration to the gown you choose. After all, it will most likely need to survive a plane trip, and your ceremony is probably planned for an unusual outdoor venue, such as on the beach or in a gazebo. You might want to forgo a grand ball gown in favor of a dress in a lighter, breezier fabric, like organza or chiffon, with a short train or no train at all. It will not only be easier to pack, but it will be better suited to the environment and style of your wedding.

*A destination dress can still be beautiful. Gown by Michelle Roth*

Weddings at a destination have become so popular that finding the right gown shouldn't be difficult. Most designers offer at least one "destination dress"— usually a simpler gown without bustles, trains, and other fussy details—in their collection.

# *Travel Tips*

Most retailers can help you find a destination-friendly gown, but it's your job to ensure it arrives safely to your wedding locale and in good condition. Make sure to:

· Pack your dress in a garment bag to prevent damage.

· Call ahead to find out whether you can hang the garment bag on the plane. If you must fold your dress, a garment bag or plastic bag will keep wrinkles to a minimum.

· Find out whether your hotel offers steaming services.

# Ethnic Wedding Gowns

Many brides want to celebrate their cultural background on this very special day, but they often want a gown that reflects their American heritage, too. The solution? "Pay tribute to both," says Brookins. For instance, Chinese brides traditionally wear red; a Chinese-American bride might wear red for the ceremony and change into a white gown for the reception. Or, she could choose a white gown with red details, like floral or Asian-inspired embroidery. An African-American bride has similar options. She could wear a white gown and incorporate a colorful patterned African fabric in a sash from a specialty designer. If you have trouble locating ethnic wedding attire in your area, you can find a variety of culturally significant wedding clothing from Internet retailers.

Your cultural heritage can add punch to a gown.
*Gown by Sincerity Bridal*

If you want to wear a traditional white gown but still want to pay homage to your cultural heritage, you can incorporate symbols of your background and your groom's into your outfit through thread or bead work. If you're Irish-American, for example, an image of a Claddagh might be embroidered on your dress or on your groom's cummerbund.

# Personal Touch

There are also details that can pay tribute to your individual style or to you and your groom as a couple. Consider having a seamstress embroider your (new) monogram on your gown's train, like Sarah Ferguson did when she married Prince Andrew. Linda Cierach, who designed Fergie's wedding dress, says that the embroidery on the gown was inspired by Sarah's family's heraldry, which is made up of thistles connected with ribbons. These were embroidered on the train, along with hearts and bumblebees that added a "sense

A dress with a difference will be memorable.
*Gown by Youlin*

of fun" unique to both Sarah and her groom, Andrew. These symbols were alternated with embroidered waves, anchors, and S's, and the whole thing culminated with "a large logo of an A with two S's," according to designer Cierach. You may not have royal heritage, but there may be symbols important to your family and to your groom's heritage that you can incorporate into your dress. These details and touches will make your gown more of an heirloom.

# Short Stuff

Today, many brides want the nontraditional look of a "playful" gown—a tea-length dress (which hits the leg mid-calf) makes it easy for brides to kick up their heels and dance. This length is also perfect for a destination wedding, second marriage, small intimate ceremony, or Vegas event. Not sure the shorter gown is appropriate for your ceremony? You might start with a traditional floor-length dress and then change for your reception.

Short is sassy.
*Dress by Watters & Watters*

Whatever look you choose for your wedding day, rest assured you really can't make a wrong decision. These days, just about anything goes—as long as you're comfortable and happy with your selection, you're sure to be a beautiful bride.

# Notes

# Notes

# Chapter Five

# *The Wedding Party*

Now that you've selected your bridal attire, you can move on to dressing those who'll be standing by your side on the Big Day—your groom, of course, along with bridesmaids, groomsmen, a flower girl, ring bearer, and any other attendants you've asked to assist and take part in the ceremony. Other important players who may need your help: your mother and father, his mother and father, stepparents . . . phew! While you're not responsible for choosing *everyone's* attire, it is important to know about proper wedding wear, so that you can offer your friends and family guidance and support.

## His Style

But before you start shopping around for bridesmaids' dresses in that perfect shade and style, take a moment to remember whose Big Day this is—not just yours, but your fiancé's, too! After your wedding-gown decisions have been made, shift your concentration over to your groom. He'll appreciate the help with all the decisions he's got to make.

The groom has nearly as many choices as the bride when it comes to selecting a suit or tuxedo, plus he gets to accessorize with his choice of tie, cummerbund, or vest, cuff links and studs. Luckily, there's no "rule" that prevents you from seeing your groom's attire ahead of time. Help him out by steering him toward the proper items to match the style and formality of your wedding. You can also help your leading man look his best by following these guidelines to flatter his figure:

| Body Type | On Top | Below |
| --- | --- | --- |
| Short and slender | Single-breasted jacket with long lines, a low-button stance to elongate the body and notch or peak lapel. Or, a double-breasted tuxedo jacket with subtly patterned vest and tie. | Reverse double-pleated trousers |
| Short, stocky, and muscular | Tuxedo jacket with slim shawl or notch lapel and natural shoulder line (avoid broad European styles). Top button should sit at the natural waist to give the torso a leaner look. | Reverse double-pleated trousers with pleats extending toward the pockets to elongate the leg. (Avoid too much of a break on the foot, or the pant leg will look sloppy.) |

| | | |
|---|---|---|
| Tall, husky, and muscular, with broad shoulders, thick neck, full face | Shawl-collar tuxedo, lay-down collar and fuller bow tie. (Avoid too-narrow ties and wing-tip collars, which look constrictive.) | Pant leg should have a slightly wider silhouette to accomodate muscular thighs. |
| Tall and slim | Longer jacket with three, four, or even five buttons. Notch or peak lapel or a double-breasted tuxedo with slightly broad shoulders and a suppressed waist. Jacket buttons closed up high on the waist-line; a high shoulder line is better than a natural one. Vests and ties in colors and patterns work well. | Trousers should have a higher rise with more of a break in the pant. |

## Does It Fit?

To ensure the best fit, a tailor should take your fiancé's measurements (whether he's buying or renting). The three measurements that ensure the best fit: overarm (around the shoulders, over the biceps, with the arms relaxed at the sides), chest (the circumference under the armpits, with the arms down at the sides), and seat (around the hips and rear—make sure your fiancé takes that wallet out of his pocket!). If the difference between your guy's coat size and waist size is 7 inches or more, he may need a made-to-measure outfit (rather than a ready-made tux). That way, he'll be able to get both trousers and jacket suited to his proportions.

To determine this, first ask yourselves, how does the tuxedo *look*? After all, measurements alone will not determine whether your guy's got the right fit. For example, his jacket sleeves should graze the fleshy part of his thumb and when his arms are at his sides, his fingertips should just touch the bottom of a traditional-length jacket. Pants should skim the hips, and the hem should break on top of the shoe. Then, ask him how he *feels* in the tuxedo. His jacket should allow for comfortable movement; trousers needn't hug too tightly at the waist. If your fiancé doesn't generally dress in formal wear (who does?), figuring out the proper fit can be confusing, but these tips should help.

Jacket: Have your fiancé place his arms at his sides and relax his hands. His fingertips should just touch the bottom of the traditional-length jacket, and his shirt cuff should extend half an inch to an inch beyond the jacket sleeve. The hem of the sleeve should graze the fleshy part of his thumb. The chest area should be roomy enough to allow easy movement. If he says the shoulders feel tight, try going up a size or experiment with another brand.

Shirt: The cuff should cover his wrist, and the neckband should be pretty roomy. To check, slip two fingers in when buttoned. Make sure the shirt cuff peeks out 1/2 inch from the jacket.

## *Keep on Tying*

Can your guy tie a standard four-in-hand tie? How about a bow tie? Most rentals come with pre-tied versions (of either style). If he wants to go the do-it-yourself route, make sure he practices or has someone do the tying on the wedding day. For a quick lesson, ask the salesperson at your tuxedo rental store.

Trousers: The fabric should skim (but not hug) the hips, and the waistline should be comfortable: not too tight and not too loose. The hem should break slightly on top of the shoe, brushing the shoelaces, and angle downward a bit in back.

---

# Dancing on Air

You're breaking in *your* shoes for a comfy first dance, right? Your fiancé should do the same, whether he's renting shoes or purchasing brand-new ones. He may not think of it, so advise him to wear them around for a while to break them in and make sure they're comfortable. Just remember to tell him the shoes should be worn indoors—not outside—so if they need to be returned, sales staff won't give him a hassle about scuffed soles. (This is only the case if the shoes are bought—rentals can be worn everywhere.)

---

Also, though the groomsmen generally dress in the same tuxedo style as the groom, your main man should make an effort to stand out somehow. He may want to wear a different but complementary vest, cummerbund, or tie (in white or ivory to coordinate with your dress, for example, while the groomsmen coordinate with the bridesmaids' colors), more extravagant cuff links and studs, or a fancier boutonniere.

# Taking Attendants

Once you've settled on your groom's wedding day attire, turn your attention to outfitting your bridal party. It's no small task, but if you've made it this far, you can tackle this, too.

# Bridesmaids

As the bride, it's your job to select dresses that will make your attendants feel comfortable and look great. "Aren't bridesmaids' dresses traditionally outdated and unflattering?" you're probably thinking. Certainly anyone with experience as an attendant can recall a wedding spent wearing a style-challenged dress that now resides in the back of a closet.

Today's designers realize there's simply no reason to make your bridesmaids look anything but beautiful. Dresses are getting more fashionable by the minute—the fabrics are elegant (think silk charmeuse, satin, or chiffon), color choices are flattering (like blues, lavenders, and corals) and many styles look like they're straight from the couture collection runways. Separates, A-line designs, and fluted skirts are among the many options now available for bridesmaids.

*Dresses by Watters & Watters*

There are plenty of styles out there that will flatter your friends—and make them *glad* they agreed to be in your wedding party. In order to find those designs, you'll have to go through some of the same steps that led you to your wedding gown. As a matter of fact, your own dress is an excellent starting point. "The bride's gown should be chosen first, always," says Mell Buonauto, co-owner of The Great White Way in Watertown, Connecticut. "Everything should be coordinated around her gown."

Why? Your wedding gown is the centerpiece that reflects the style, theme, and formality of your celebration, so naturally, bridesmaids' outfits should complement these elements. Create a unified look by selecting bridesmaids' dresses that incorporate details of your gown, such as beadwork or embroidery. Or, have everyone—including you—wear the same style of jewelry, gloves, or other accessories.

When considering the style of dress you'd like your bridesmaids to wear, take into account their different heights, skin tones, and personal styles—just like you did when selecting your own gown. Bright fuchsia may not be the best choice if one of your bridesmaids has pink-toned skin and flaming red hair, for example. ("Nutmeg, a deep brownish tone, works great for redheads," advises Yolanda Cellucci, of Yolanda's in Waltham, Massachusetts.)

Also, you may want to tone down the colors and variety of styles among your bridesmaids, in order to shine as the star of this

## Who Pays?

Good news, it's not you! Bridesmaids are responsible for purchasing their own gowns, accessories, and shoes—which means a considerate bride-to-be will try to keep costs down. Don't forget, these maids will be throwing you a shower, buying you gifts, and, perhaps, funding a bachelorette party in your honor, so it's only right you don't send them into debt with their dress purchase (plus, some attendants might incur travel costs in order to be in your wedding). If you have your heart set on a particular but expensive dress, consider offering to chip in to offset the cost as a gift to your bridesmaids for being in the wedding.

show, says Buonauto. "Bridesmaids' dresses are the background," she explains. "They're the canvas for the picture—you."

Think about body types. Are your maids a matched set of "triangles" or "rectangles," or do you have a variety of sizes and shapes to consider? Most likely, your friends' figures aren't identical, so finding a single dress that flatters all of them will be a challenge. For instance, your petite, small-shouldered pal won't be any happier wearing an off-the-shoulder style than your full-figured friend will be in a strapless sheath. Also, you don't want to force your attendants to wear dresses that make them feel self-conscious or uncomfortable. After all, these are some of your best friends and favorite relatives—you'll want them to feel pretty and confident as they help celebrate your wedding day.

If the whole process sounds daunting and stressful, there's one obvious solution: give your bridesmaids some say in choosing the style they'll wear. Let them narrow the options; you make the final decision. Or, select a variety of styles and colors (with assistance from your trusted maid of honor and mom, perhaps) then ask your bridal party to select their favorite.

## Mix 'n' Match

Picture the traditional wedding party photo of years past and what do you see? Bridesmaids dressed in identical dresses, wearing identical hairstyles, and donning identical accessories. Luckily, today there are other options available. And when you have a variety of shapes, sizes, and complexions to consider, it may be simpler—and wiser—to opt for bridesmaids' gowns that *aren't* exactly the same, but still match in color or style. Separates are a great solution, offering the options of several different tops and skirts that may all be similar (in hue or fabric), but still reflect varied styles and flatter different body types. They also provide a more interesting visual effect for your guests.

As the bride, you get to set the rules—which means you can do whatever works best for you and your bridal party. A few ideas:

• Find a dress you like and choose a color, then let bridesmaids select from the available styles within the same collection.

# *Bridesmaids Behaving Badly*

Your bridal party should be a collection of the closest, most supportive women in your life—you can count on them to drop everything when it comes to planning your wedding, right? Well, no. Fact is, a bridesmaid could easily find herself in a career crisis just when you'd like her to help shop for dresses. She might have a vacation planned for the week you want her measurements taken. She could meet the man of her dreams—and become completely preoccupied—right when you need her to start scheduling fittings.

While you can't expect everyone's undivided attention, a little prodding isn't out of order when bridesmaids aren't cooperative. Feel free to call and (nicely) explain your concerns. Offer to make things easier: perhaps your friend could call in her measurements from another shop closer to her home or work. Or, you might be able to help her reorganize her schedule and find time for fittings.

If you find yourself dealing with a truly unenthusiastic attendant, give her a gracious way out of your wedding. Explain simply that you realize she can't find the time, you understand if she wants to back out, and you'll miss her if she does. If she stays, she'll have a clearer idea of what is expected, and if she goes, you're free to choose a more enthusiastic, helpful friend to take her place as a bridesmaid. Either way, you can't lose.

- Select a standard element, such as a black ball gown skirt, then have attendants choose their tops in a choice of complementary shades. Or select separates in a particular color and fabric, and let each bridesmaid choose a top and bottom from that particular collection.

- Decide on the dress style, but offer bridesmaids a choice of two complementary colors.

# Gown Grief

*Q* *One of my bridesmaids hates the dress I've selected, but I don't want to change it since everyone else loves it—including me! What should I tell her?*

*A* Since screaming "It's my wedding, and you'll wear what I want you to wear!" is not an option, you'll have to use a little diplomacy. First, try to find out what it is she dislikes about your selection. Is it the strapless style? If so, ask your salon about a coordinating shawl or stole. The color? Tell her how it brings out her eyes (flattery works!). If you can't sway her opinion, consider compromising on the issue. You might allow her to wear a gown in a different color or length, for example, if you can convince a few other bridesmaids to do the same for visual balance.

On the other hand, accommodating one difficult bridesmaid may be too much stress to handle. As the bride, you have the final word on what your attendants wear, and if you put it gracefully, you may just get your way without too much fuss. Tell your friend she looks beautiful in the dress, it would mean a lot to you if she would wear it, and you'll never forget her gracious concession if she does. If that doesn't work, let her know—calmly and kindly—that she's free to step down from her duties.

- Keep it simple, and let bridesmaids wear formal black dresses in whatever style they want. (Theoretically, this idea can work with any color, but it may be trickier to match varying shades of red, purple, green, etc.)

Even if your bridesmaids aren't dressed in identical gowns, you can still ask them to wear similar jewelry, such as a pearl necklace and earrings. As for dictating hairstyles and makeup? Sorry, that's taking your authority a bit too far!

# Little Women

*Q  I'd like to include my ten-year-old niece in the bridal party, but she's too young to be a bridesmaid and too old to be a flower girl. What should I do?*

*A*  Consider making her a junior bridesmaid. These helpers are usually between the ages of 8 and sixteen, so your niece fits perfectly in this role. Her duties are similar to those of an older bridesmaid—she attends the ceremony rehearsal (and dinner with her parents if they choose) and walks in the processional on your wedding day. However, she will not be expected to help your other bridesmaids throw a shower or contribute to their gift to you (unless her parents want to do so on her behalf) or stand in the receiving line after the ceremony. Junior bridesmaids who are at the older end of the age range (about 15 or 16) usually wear the same dress as the older bridesmaids. The same style might not suit a junior bridesmaid who is on the younger side, however. In that case, select a dress style that's the same color as your bridesmaids' gowns (so she'll feel included) but isn't too sophisticated for a child.

Remember, there are no hard and fast rules when it comes to dressing your bridesmaids, and the best approach is to do what's most comfortable for you *and* them. If your bridesmaids are similar in body type and personal style, for example, then the same dress style for all may not be a problem. But have each one select her own shoes and accessories to keep the cookie-cutter effect in check. Giving bridesmaids free reign in choosing what they wear is fine, provided the dresses they select reflect your gown in style and formality.

## Dollars & Sense

No need to break your bridesmaids' budgets. Keep expenses at a reasonable level with these tips:

- Defray costs to bridesmaids by offering to pay the deposit on their gowns as your gift to them.

- Consider purchasing bridesmaids' dresses at the same shop where you bought your gown—some stores give discounts for multiple orders.

- Don't limit yourself to bridal shops when searching for bridesmaids' dresses. Department stores stock styles that are just as formal—and may cost less. And be sure to check the end-of-season sales rack! (But remember that with a department store purchase, you're taking the risk that a guest may wind up dressed the same as your bridesmaids.)

# Style Guide

No matter the time of day, these guidelines will help you select appropriate bridesmaids' outfits.

## Daytime Weddings (before 6 P.M.)

**Ultra-Formal**  Long dresses and shoes to match; gloves and jeweled combs or other hair accessories are optional.

**Formal**  Long or short dresses and shoes to match; hair accessories and gloves are optional.

**Semiformal**  Long or short dresses and shoes to match; hair accessories are optional.

**Informal**  Only the maid of honor is dressed in a short dress or suit, similar in style to the bride's attire.

## Evening Weddings (after 6 P.M.)

**Ultra-Formal**  Long dresses and shoes to match; jeweled combs or other hair accessories; gloves are optional.

**Formal**  Long or tea-length dresses and shoes to match; hair accessories and gloves are optional.

**Semiformal**  Floor, tea-length, or shorter dresses and shoes to match; hair accessories are optional.

**Informal**  Only the maid of honor is dressed in a short dress or suit, similar in style to the bride's attire.

# Bridesmaids' Worksheet

Keep track of bridesmaids' attire with this worksheet.

### Dresses

Individual price _____

Manufacture _____

Color _____

Store _____

Contact _____

Telephone number _____

Date ordered _____

Date of first fitting _____

Date of second fitting _____

Delivery date _____

### Hair Accessories

Individual price _____

Manufacturer _____

Store _____

Contact _____

Telephone number _____

Quantity ordered _____

Date ordered _____

Delivery date _____

### Shoes

Individual price _____

Manufacturer _____

Color _____

Store _____

Telephone number _____

Pairs ordered _____

Date ordered _____

Delivery date _____

## Gloves

Price per pair _____

Manufacturer _____

Store _____

Telephone number _____

Pairs ordered _____

Date ordered _____

Delivery date _____

## Accessories

Individual price _____

Items _____

Manufacturer _____

Store _____

Telephone number _____

Quantity ordered _____

Date ordered _____

Delivery date _____

# Groomsmen

Just as the bridesmaids' dresses reflect the style and formality of your gown, the groomsmen's formal wear should echo your groom's attire, whether they're dressed in identical outfits right down to the shoes or the groom stands out with distinguishing touches, such as a different color tie and vest or cummerbund. Most grooms simply rent (or purchase) a tuxedo, and their groomsmen do the same, selecting the same style by the same manufacturer. They can even choose matching shoes to achieve a completely uniform look. And, like the bridesmaids, groomsmen are also responsible for the cost of their own attire.

## *Return to Sender*

"Where's my shirt?" "Whose tie is this?" Your fiancé may want to help out his buddies by appointing the best man or another attendant to gather all rented items and return them to the store after the wedding.

Of course, there are certain elements of the formal wear ensemble that do have to be carefully selected—and here's where you may want to voice your opinion. In addition to the formal shirt, jacket, and trousers, groomsmen also wear a tie with a vest or cummerbund that should coordinate with your bridesmaids' dresses in color and style. In addition, the men should don cuff links and studs. Before leaving the store, they'd be wise to try on every element—right down to the cuff links, studs, and shoes. That way, they'll be sure the outfit is complete and everything fits the way it should.

# *Military Man*

If you're marrying a member of the military, he may want to wear his uniform on your wedding day—and who could object to that? If some attendants are servicemen and some are not, you could ask them all to dress in traditional formal wear to create a unified effect. However, it is perfectly acceptable to have some groomsmen in uniform (those who are enlisted, on active duty, retired, or at a military academy as a cadet or official) and the rest in traditional formal wear. Brides who are in the military may also opt for full dress uniform rather than a gown.

## Guy Style

Like bridesmaids, groomsmen should dress to match the style and formality of your wedding. Follow these guidelines to find the proper attire for your groomsmen, whether they'll be dressed in traditional tuxedos or more contemporary wear.

### *Daytime Weddings (before 6 P.M.)*

**Ultra-Formal**    *Traditional:* cutaway suit with striped trousers and a wing-collar shirt.

*Contemporary:* long or short contoured tuxedo with formal trousers and a wing-collar shirt.

**Formal**    *Traditional:* stroller, waistcoat, striped trousers, white shirt, and striped tie.

*Contemporary:* formal tuxedo, dress shirt, bow or four-in-hand tie, vest or cummerbund.

**Semiformal** *Traditional:* suit with a white, colored, or striped shirt and four-in-hand tie.

*Contemporary:* dinner jacket or formal suit, dress shirt, bow or four-in-hand tie, vest or cummerbund.

**Informal** *Traditional:* suit with a white, colored, or striped shirt and four-in-hand tie.

*Contemporary:* dinner jacket or formal suit, dress shirt, bow or four-in-hand tie, vest.

## Evening Weddings (after 6 P.M.)

**Ultra-Formal** *Traditional:* full-dress tailcoat, matching trousers, white waistcoat, white bow tie, wing-collar shirt.

*Contemporary:* long or short contoured tuxedo with formal trousers and wing-collar shirt.

**Formal** *Traditional:* stroller, waistcoat, striped trousers, white shirt, striped tie.

*Contemporary:* formal tuxedo, dress shirt, bow or four-in-hand tie, vest or cummerbund.

**Semiformal** *Traditional:* white or colored suit, striped shirt, and four-in-hand tie.

*Contemporary:* dinner jacket or formal suit, dress shirt, bow or four-in-hand tie, vest or cummerbund.

**Informal** *Traditional:* suit with a white, colored, or striped shirt, four-in-hand tie.

*Contemporary:* dinner jacket or formal suit, dress shirt, bow or four-in-hand tie, vest or cummerbund.

# Gender Bending

 *Our best man is a woman. What should she wear?*

This situation is more common than ever before, with many couples today selecting nontraditional bridal parties. There are several options available for a woman serving in this role. Since she should stand out as the groom's honor attendant, she could wear a gown of her own choosing, or, if you want her to match your bridesmaids, she could wear the same style dress in a different color. Another option: ask her to match the groomsmen in a black or navy dress with white gloves. (On the flip side, if a male friend stands up for the bride, he should wear a tuxedo in the same style as the groomsmen; his shirt color, tie, vest, or cummerbund can match the bridesmaids' dress color.)

Flowers can also help distinguish your "best woman's" special place in the ceremony. While bridesmaids might carry a bouquet and groomsmen will wear boutonnieres, she could have a wrist corsage instead.

Selecting a female friend for this role is a nontraditional, creative choice for your wedding—so don't be afraid to get creative with her attire, too!

# Style Guide

Don't know what a wing collar looks like? Never heard of a stroller (no, not the kind babies use!)? If you don't know what to look for, you'll have a pretty tough time finding it in the store. Sales staff can help, of course, but why not become a pro yourself with this dictionary of men's formal wear terms.

## SUIT STYLES

**Cutaway/morning coat:** Tapers from the front waist button to a long, wide back tail. Accessorize with a wing-collar shirt with an ascot and coordinated vest. Worn with matching striped trousers. Comes in black or gray.

Cutaway/ morning coat

**Stroller/walking coat:** Cut slightly longer than a regular suit jacket. Worn with a laydown collar shirt, four-in-hand tie, and matching striped trousers. Comes in black or gray.

**Dinner suit:** A white or ivory jacket with black formal trousers worn in warm weather for formal and semiformal evening weddings.

Tuxedo Jacket

**Tuxedo:** A single- or double-breasted jacket with matching trousers for formal or semiformal evening weddings. Accessorize with a dress shirt, with cuff links and studs, a bow tie or four-in-hand, and a vest or cummerbund.

**White tie:** A tailcoat jacket in black or white, short in front with two long back tails. Worn with a wing-collar shirt with a white piqué (a waffle-textured cotton or cotton blend fabric) bib, tie, and vest.

White tie

## LAPELS

**Notch:** Triangular indentation where the lapel joins the collar.

**Peak:** Broad, V-shaped, points up and out just below the collar line.

**Shawl:** Smooth, rounded lapel.

Peak lapel with band collar shirt

## SHIRTS

**Band collar:** Stands up around the neck; typically worn without a tie and closed with a decorative collar button that matches the shirt studs.

**Classic:** Traditional formal white shirt, often pleated on either side of the buttons or studs; may or may not have French cuffs.

**Laydown collar:** Folds over around the neck with a wide division between points in front (similar to a standard button-front shirt).

**Wing collar:** A stiff band encircles the neck with turned-down points ("the wings") in front.

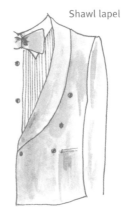

Shawl lapel

Wing collar

Classic collar

## TIES

**Ascot or cravat:** A wide necktie looped over and held in place under the chin with a tie tack or stickpin; worn with a wing-collar shirt, a daytime wedding cutaway jacket, or a traditional tuxedo.

**Bow:** Tied in the shape of a bow; worn with a wing or laydown collar shirt; available in a variety of widths, colors, and patterns to match the vest or cummerbund.

**Euro:** A long, knotted, square-bottom necktie; worn with a wing or laydown collar shirt and a vest.

**Four-in-hand:** A standard, long knotted necktie; worn with a laydown collar shirt and a vest.

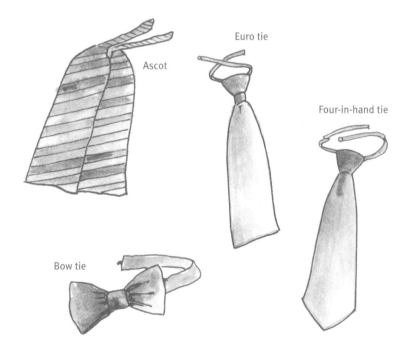

Ascot

Euro tie

Four-in-hand tie

Bow tie

## *Don't Forget!*

Groomsmen who think they have it easy sometimes overlook the most obvious element of formal attire—black dress socks. They'll have to supply their own, and white sweat socks will *not* do in a pinch. Your groom may want to keep a few extra pairs on hand for his buddies on your wedding day.

### ACCESSORIES

**Cuff links and studs:** Decorative jewelry used to close cuffs and button formal shirts.

**Cummerbund:** A pleated silk or satin sash worn at the waist that covers the trousers' waistband. Worn with bow tie only, never with a four-in-hand tie.

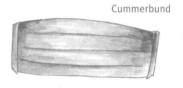

Cummerbund

**Pocket square:** A small pocket handkerchief matching the vest and tie fabric, tucked into the left breast pocket; can be worn by groomsmen instead of boutonnieres.

**Suspenders:** Two supporting bands worn over the shoulders to support the trousers; coordinated in color or pattern with the cummerbund.

**Vest:** Worn in place of a cummerbund to cover the trousers' waistband; may have a full back or be adjustable at the neck and waist with an open back; often worn with a coordinating four-in-hand or bow tie.

# Groomsmen's Worksheet

Keep track of groomsmen's attire with this worksheet.

Store _____

Telephone _____

Tuxedo manufacturer _____

Date ordered _____ Pickup date _____

Down-payment amount _____

Balance due date _____

Return date _____

Coat _____ Style # _____

Individual price _____

Trousers _____ Style # _____

Individual price _____

Shirt _____ Style # _____

Individual price _____

Shoes _____ Style # _____

Individual price _____

Accessories _____

Item(s) _____

Price _____

# Mothers of the Bride and Groom

Although it's certainly not up to you to decide how your mother and mother-in-law-to-be should dress on your wedding day, don't be surprised if they ask for your assistance. After all, each mom will

## Dress Distress

**Q** *My mother-in-law (to be) showed me her dress for our wedding yesterday. It's way too informal! How can I convince her to wear something more appropriate for the formal ceremony and reception my fiancé and I have planned?*

**A** While you can't exercise the same authority here as you can with your bridesmaids, you *can* make recommendations to help guarantee that both of you will be comfortable with her attire on your wedding day. After all, your mother-in-law probably doesn't *want* to be dressed inappropriately—she may not realize just how formal your celebration is going to be. Talk to her about the style of gowns you've chosen for your attendants, and if your mother is wearing a dress you like, describe it—or show it—to your mother-in-law. You can even make subtle suggestions that she reconsider the dress she showed you in favor of a different style. ("Yes, that certainly is a gorgeous dress for a wedding! I should probably tell you, however, I wore a short, strapless style like that once and found it wasn't so easy to dance in.") Still, don't force the issue. If she chooses to wear the original dress, respect her decision. After all, she knows what sort of attire will make her feel best on the Big Day, and she's entitled to wear what she wants—just like you!

want to look special for this momentous occasion—she'll likely fret over finding that perfect dress in just the right color to convey her important role in your day. Plus, she'll also want to complement—though not exactly match—the other mother's outfit.

Traditionally, the bride's mother has first dibs on what to wear. She chooses a gown, then calls up the groom's mom to describe the dress (color, style, etc.), thus ensuring they won't wind up either a) clashing, or b) looking like identical twins. However, if your mothers aren't close, this may not happen naturally. That's where you come in. Communicate for both moms, offering helpful suggestions—and hints—if you're so inclined.

Speaking of mothers, you may be wondering what to do about stepmothers. If there are any stepmothers involved in your wedding, it's a good idea to make sure they're aware of the gown choices your mother and your groom's mother have made. Remember, it's not up to you to decide how their attire should compare in terms of formality or style, and you don't have to get caught in the middle of any disputes. Just make a few phone calls so everyone is up to speed.

# Father's Day

Don't forget that the father of the bride plays a prominent fashion role in the wedding, too! If yours is a traditional ceremony, he'll walk you down the aisle dressed similarly to the groomsmen, which usually means a matching tuxedo.

If you have a stepfather who will be involved in the ceremony, he should also dress like the groomsmen. If he will be present but not involved, formal attire is not necessary, and he may choose to wear attire more like the guests.

For the father of the groom, formal attire is appropriate whether or not he is directly involved in the ceremony.

# Child's Play

Planning to include little ones in your ceremony? Flower girls and ring bearers are traditionally between four and eight years old and they, too, should be dressed in styles and colors to coordinate with the rest of your wedding party.

A ring bearer will look adorable in a child-sized suit or a tuxedo that matches the groomsmen's. But when it comes to outfitting young female attendants, you certainly don't have to dress them like child brides or miniature bridesmaids. Traditional attire for the flower girl: a dress with a full skirt and pouf sleeves in white, off-white, soft pastel colors, or a shade that complements your bridal party. (Just be sure the hem isn't so long she can't walk comfortably—you don't want her tripping down the aisle.) Or, accessorize her hair with ribbons and bows in the same color as the bridesmaids' dresses.

Many bridal shops and formal wear retailers offer a selection that's just right for children; special occasion children's wear can also be found at most major department stores and specialty children's clothing shops.

# Notes

# Notes

# Notes

*Chapter Six*

# *Retiring Your Attire*

When your wedding is over, you'll have plenty of mementos to remember your Big Day: photos, video, a slice of wedding cake saved to eat on your first anniversary, and, of course, that gorgeous wedding gown. So how best to preserve your dress for posterity?

It's not likely you'll be wearing it again—even if you and your husband decide to celebrate one day with a second wedding—so you'll need to decide what to do with it. You may want to store it for your future daughter to wear, or you may choose to sell it, donate it, or find another use for this dream dress. If you're planning to keep the gown, you must give it special care.

## Laundry Day

Before you store your gown, make sure to have it professionally cleaned—even if it doesn't look dirty. As you may know from examining your mother's wedding dress, old stains are difficult to remove, and some spills don't show up right away. The sugars in white wine turn brown with time, but initially there's hardly a noticeable spot. Other culprits: perspiration and oil from lotions or perfumes, which can also turn to stains later on.

# Taking It to the Cleaners

 *I think I've found a good cleaner. How can I be sure?*

"It's very important not to presume that because somebody cleans sweaters they're able to clean gowns," says Steven Saidman, a gown preservationist. "This is a specialty, and wedding gowns have to be handled properly."

Ask tons of questions! Find out how long the cleaner has been in business (preferably long enough to have experience with a variety of gown fabrics). Make sure you won't be asked to sign anything releasing the cleaner from responsibility in case of damage, and find out about the warranty, which should allow you to inspect your gown after preservation and should state a specific number of years the warranty covers. Also, get a guarantee that hidden stains will be removed and that preservation boxes and other materials will be safe for your dress.

Ask about price. Saidman says reputable cleaners charge different prices depending on the work required, rather than a flat rate (which indicates your dress won't get any special treatment); you'll also want to clarify whether that price includes bridal accessories. If your cleaner passes this game of 20 Questions, it should be safe letting him handle your dress!

Whatever you do, don't attempt to remove stains or clean the dress in any way yourself! Instead, ask recently married friends to recommend a good gown preservation service or a professional cleaner who specializes in wedding gowns. Before handing over your dress, feel free to check out the company with the Better Business Bureau. Also, discuss the cleaning process with your cleaner. Find out whether your gown can be dry-cleaned safely; some fabrics and details need to be professionally hand-washed (again, don't try this at home). According to Steven Saidman, co-owner of Imperial Gown Restoration and Preservation Company based in Fairfax, Virginia, dry cleaners aren't always your best bet since they don't necessarily specialize in cleaning and preserving wedding gowns. Be certain the cleaner you choose will use stain pretreatments, fresh dry-cleaning fluid (if it's to be dry-cleaned), and a mesh bag for protection. You may sound high-maintenance, but why risk taking a chance with your wedding dress?

At home, examine your dress for visible spots, especially at the hem and on the train. Mend any tears and reinforce loose details (or take it to a tailor for more major repairs). When you're ready to drop it off, point out any stains and, if you can, tell your cleaner what caused them—this will make his job easier when he tries to remove them.

## Box It Up

Once your dress has been cleaned, you'll need to store it properly. Hanging your gown isn't advised—over time, the dress will stretch at the shoulders. Rather, have it boxed professionally. A cleaner who specializes in wedding gowns should be able to preserve your dress properly, by cleaning with stain pretreatments, fresh cleaning fluid, and a mesh bag for protection; hand-pressing the dress (meaning it's pressed by hand inside and out); then storing in an acid-free or certified pH-neutral box. Your cleaner should also be able to offer you a warranty. The cost for all of this: anywhere from $150 to $700, with warranties commonly ranging from 20 to 50 years.

Is the cost worth it if you only paid $300 for your dress? Yes, says Saidman. "The value of the gown is not in what you paid for it. It's an investment you made in a dress you love." Consider this: You may want to pass this gown on to your daughter one day. Saving a few hundred dollars now may not mean much if you later find the dress didn't survive over time.

You also have the option of preserving the dress yourself. It isn't hard, but it is important to do it right, starting with letting a professional handle the cleaning and hand-pressing. (Keep in mind, you won't have that warranty, and you aren't likely to save much money—cleaning alone might cost about $350.)

## What you'll need:

- An acid-free container large enough to hold your gown without crushing it (see **Resources** for vendors)

- Two clean white bedsheets

- Acid-free white tissue paper (see **Resources** for vendors)

Begin by lining the container with one of the sheets, so your dress won't directly touch the sides of the container. Next, remove the dry cleaner's plastic bag and get to work on the dress. Certain details will deteriorate over time, so they'll need to be removed and stored separately: fabric-covered metal buttons, metal fasteners, pins, and sponge or foam shoulder pads.

Fold the gown, and place it gently in the container—don't put it back in the plastic bag. Creating some creases is okay. "They'll steam right out in the future," explains Saidman.

Use the acid-free tissue paper to stuff pouf sleeves and other shaped areas of the dress. You can also lay tissue paper in the gown's folds to lessen creasing—there will still be some, but without the tissue the folds will become set. Finally, cover the dress with the second white sheet, then cover with the box lid.

Now the big question is, where will you store it? Don't even think about the attic or basement—temperature changes here will be too extreme and the atmosphere may be damp. Instead, choose a cool, dry area, such as under your bed (provided you don't have a curious cat) or at the top of a hall closet. Be sure the gown will not be exposed to light, dust, or insects.

Miss your dress already? Check on it periodically—even if it's stored in the most secure area of your house. It's actually good for your gown: "Sealed boxes do not protect textiles," explains Saidman. "A gown needs to breathe, and it's light that is damaging to fabrics, not air."

If you find signs of discoloration, mildew, or pest infestation, contact your dry cleaner or bridal salon quickly for advice—before the damage is too great.

# Recycle and Reuse

Of course, storing your dress for potential reuse in the future isn't your only option. Some brides opt to turn the gown into something useful almost immediately after the wedding. While it's nearly impossible to have a wedding dress tailored for other formal occasions (it will *always* look like a wedding gown), it is quite possible to use portions of the material in creative ways. Examples: Have a dress made from your wedding gown material for your future child's christening or communion; include bits of your dress fabric in a quilt or a pillow covering.

# On Sale Now

Hoping to recoup a portion of your gown's cost by selling it to another excited bride-to-be? As you know from your own search for that perfect gown, consignment shops often sell secondhand wedding dresses. Check the Yellow Pages and call around to see if they'll accept yours—many shops take only seasonal items and some are even more selective about the clothing they'll agree to sell.

Consignment shops usually charge a small drop-off fee, then keep the dress in the store for a limited time. When you drop off the gown, you'll be asked what you'd like to do if it doesn't sell. Options usually include picking up the gown to take home or allowing the shop to donate it. Be sure to get everything you agree to in writing before leaving the store.

You can also try selling the dress yourself through a newspaper ad or online auction such as eBay, Yahoo! Auctions (auctions.yahoo.com) or sell.com. Set a reasonable price (high enough to allow for bargaining, but lower than the price *you* paid) and wait for the calls and e-mails to come in!

# Donation Frocks

Another way to pass on the goodwill: Donate your dress. Although you may initially think you spent too much money on the gown to just give it away, remember that items gifted to charity are tax deductible (be sure to get a receipt), and they're always appreciated.

All sorts of organizations resell donated wedding gowns with specific plans for the proceeds they'll gain from the sale. Search the Internet for the charity of your choice. For example, the Salvation Army accepts wedding gowns to resell at drastically reduced prices to brides who might not be able to afford a dress otherwise. Items sold at the Army's thrift stores benefit more than 120 adult rehabilitation centers nationwide. For more information, go to www.salvationarmyusa.org. Investigate shops in your area that donate proceeds to charity or nonprofit organizations. Dresses donated to The Bridal Garden in New York City, for example, help Sheltering Arms Children's Services to provide day care, foster care, adoption, and special education, after-school, and summer programs to 3,000 New York City children. For more information, call 212-213-6071 or go to www.bridalgarden.org. Making Memories Breast Cancer Foundation sells donated gowns nationwide to raise money to raise awareness of breast cancer and to help breast cancer patients fulfill a dream or wish. For more information, call 503-252-3955 or go to www.makingmemories.org.

Once you've identified a charity you're interested in helping out, dig a little deeper. Find out how long the organization has been around and what percentage of the proceeds will actually go toward your cause. Also, ask whether they'll take care of cleaning costs or whether you should have your dress cleaned before donating it.

# Resources

## Wedding Gown Retailers, National

**David's Bridal**
More than 190 locations throughout
the continental U.S.
888-480-BRIDE
www.davidsbridal.com

**Group USA**
More than 13 locations throughout
the continental U.S.
877-867-7600
www.groupUSA.com

**Jessica McClintock**
More than 45 locations throughout
the continental U.S.
www.jessicamcclintock.co

**Priscilla of Boston**
More than 10 locations throughout
the continental U.S.
800-970-9205
www.priscillaofboston.co

**Saks Fifth Avenue**
More than 11 locations throughout
the continental U.S.
877-551-SAKS
www.saksfifthave.com

## Wedding Gown Retailers, by State

### ALABAMA

**Debra Porter**
4800 Company Road 85
Fayette, AL 35555
205-932-5212

**Jim Massey Formals & Bridal**
531 E. South Street
Montgomery, AL 36104
334-794-2669

**Minton's Bridals and Formals**
281 S. McGregory Avenue
Mobile, AL 36608
251-342-2543
www.mintonsonline.com

**Tang's**
500 Cloverdale Road
Montgomery, AL 36106
334-263-9584
www.suetang.com

**The Something Blue Shop**
224 Main Street
Hartselle, AL 35640
256-773-4956

### ARKANSAS

**Low's Bridal & Formal**
127 W. Cedar Street
Brinkley, AR 72021
870-734-3244
www.lowsbridal.com

**Today's Bride & Formalwear**
318 S. First Street
Rogers, AR 72756
479-631-7800

**Bridals by Franca**
11725 N. 19th Avenue
Suite 9
Phoenix, AZ 85029
602-943-7973

**Margot Alexis Bridal**
15848 East Jericho Drive
Fountain Hills, AZ 85268
480-951-4009

**Bay Area Bridal**
10123 North Wolfe Road
Cupertino, CA 95014
408-517-5700
www.bayareabridal.net

**Bianca's Bridal**
1700 McHenry Avenue
Suite 36
Modesto, CA 95350
209-575-5902

**Bridal & Veil**
1233 Camino Del Rio South
San Diego, CA 92108
619-295-0820
www.brideamerica.com

**Bridal Mart Factory Outlet**
2801 Prospect Park
Rancho Cordova, CA 95670
916-635-9333
www.bridalmegamall.com

**Castle for Brides**
15091 Golden West Street
Huntington Beach, CA 92647
714-891-6800

**Celebration Bridal**
2325 Palos Verdes Drive West, Suite 220
Palos Verdes Estates, CA 90274
310-265-7117
www.weddingchannel.com/ca/
celebration.com

**Gesinee's Bridal**
2368 Concord Boulevard
Concord, CA 94520
925-686-6444
www.gesineesbridal.com

**Gilda's Bridal Touch**
1305 Cleveland Avenue
Santa Rosa, CA 95401
707-566-0425

**Grace Couture Bridal**
3600 Sacramento Street
San Francisco, CA 94118
415-771-7875
www.gracecouture.com

**Ladies and Gents Bridal**
124 Oak Street
Bakersfield, CA 93304
661-325-7911

**Lili Bridals & Formals**
18663 Ventura Boulevard
Tarzana, CA 91356
818-774-9700
www.lilibridals.com

**Marina Morrison Ltd.**
30 Maiden Lane
San Francisco, CA 94108
415-984-9360
www.marinamorrison.com

**Mon Amie Bridal Salon**
355 S. Bristol Street
Costa Mesa, CA 92626
714-546-5700
www.monamie.com

**New Things West**
10123 North Wolfe Road
Cupertino, CA 95014
408-517-5711
www.newthings.com

**R-Mine Bridal Couture**
413 East Glenoaks Boulevard
Glendale, CA 91207
818-247-8177
www.rminebridal.com

**The Unique Bride**
1209 Howard Avenue
Burlingame, CA 94010
650-347-7001
www.uniquebride.com

**Trudy's**
134 The Prune Yard
Campbell, CA 95008
408-377-1987
www.trudysbrides.com

COLORADO

**Auer's**
210 Saint Paul Street
Denver, CO 80206
303-321-0404
www.auers.com

**D'Anelli Bridals**
7301 West Alameda Avenue
Suite E
Lakewood, CO 80226
303-980-1400

**The Bridal Collection**
8101 E. Belleview Avenue
Suite A-60
Denver, CO 80237
720-493-9454
www.coloradobridalcollection.com

**Vows**
522 Kimbark
Longmount, CO 80501
303-776-3103

CONNECTICUT

**Fairy Tales Formal Wear & Bridal Boutique**
125 Lebanon Avenue
Colchester, CT 06415
860-537-0886

**Josie Bridal Salon**
515 Bridge Point Avenue
Shelton, CT 06484
203-226-5811

**Julie Allen Bridals**
154 South Main Street
Newton, CT 06470
203-426-4378

**Marie's Bridal Shoppe, Ltd.**
2337 Black Rock Turnpike
Fairfield, CT 06825
203-372-5712
www.mariesbridal.com

**Mariella Creations, Inc.**
2192 Silas Deanne Highway
Rocky Hill, CT 06067
860-529-8558

DELAWARE

**Bridal and Tuxedo Outlet**
Astro Shopping Center
Kirkwood Highway
Newark, DE 18711
302-731-8802

**Candlelight Bridal & Formal**
314 Main Street
Millsboro, DE 19966
302-934-8009

**Simon's Bridal Shoppe**
215 West Loockerman
Dover, DE 19904
800-876-3152
www.simonsbridal.com

**Taylor's Bridal Boutique**
724 Philadelphia Pike
Wilmington, DE 19809
302-764-6440

FLORIDA

**A Beautiful Bride**
69 C1 South Dixie Highway
St. Augustine, FL 32084
904-826-3366

**Alegria's Brides**
130 Miracle Mile
Coral Gables, FL 33134
305-448-0699
www.alegriasbrides.com

**Aurora Unique Bridal Boutique**
1697 N. Wickham Road
Melbourne, FL 32935
321-254-3880
www.aurorabridal.com

**Bridal Concepts & Formalwear**
9140 Seminole Boulevard
Seminole, FL 33772
727-398-1111

**Bridal Suite**
1020 Port St. Lucie Boulevard
Port St. Lucie, FL 34952
772-335-5500

**Chic Parisien**
118 Miracle Mile
Coral Gables, FL 33134
305-448-5756

**The Collection for Stepping Out**
301 Park Avenue North
Winter Park, FL 32789
407-740-6003
www.thecollectionbridal.com

**Elva's for the Bride**
199 West Palmetto Park Road
Boca Raton, FL 33432
561-392-1417
www.debmccoy.com

**Ever After Formal Wear, Inc.**
9484 S. Orange Blossom Trail
Orlando, FL 32837
407-854-0259
www.everafterformal.com

**Forever Formal**
87042 Saxon Boulevard
Orange City, FL 32763
386-775-1800
www.foreverformal.com

**Forever Formal**
2900 South Nova Road, #1
Daytona Beach, FL 32119
386-760-3777
www.foreverformal.com

**Jill Stevens**
8653-1 Bay Meadows Road
Jacksonville, FL 32256
904-731-7977

**Siboney Bridal Fashions**
8001 South Orange Blossom Trail
Suite 792
Orlando, FL 32809
407-857-7400
www.siboneybridal.com

**The Studio Bridal Couture Gallery**
541 North Monroe Street
Tallahassee, FL 32301
850-222-4888

Georgia

**Belles & Beaus Bridal**
282 Hwy 314
Fayetteville, GA 30214
770-461-4818
www.belles-beaus.com

**Bridal Mart of Savannah**
11 Gateway Boulevard South
Savannah, GA 31419
912-927-8888
www.bridalmartofsavannah.com

**Bridals by Lori**
6021 Sandy Springs Circle
Atlanta, GA 30328
404-252-8767
www.bridalsbylori.com

**Bride Beautiful**
6690 Roswell Road
Atlanta, GA 30328
404-250-4330
www.bridebeautifulinc.com

**The House of the Bride**
338 Greene Street
Augusta, GA 30901
706-722-1196

**New Natalie's Bridals**
919 Chattahoochee Avenue
Atlanta, GA 30318
404-352-1616
www.newnataliesbridals.com

ILLINOIS

**A L'Amour**
236 W. Northwest Highway
Barrington, IL 60010-3195
847-381-5858

**Alessandra Bridal**
3748 W. 26th Street
Chicago, IL 60623
773-542-4146
www.alessandrabridal.com

**Bridal Elegance**
205 West Etna Road
Ottawa, IL 61350
815-433-3050

**Formals of Litchfield**
913 W. Union Avenue
Litchfield, IL 62056
888-324-4513
www.myformals.com

**Ultimate Bride**
106 East Oak Street
Chicago, IL 60610
312-337-6300

**Vera's House of Bridals**
1781 South Bell School Road
Rockford, IL 61016
815-332-5585

**Volles Bridal**
53 South Old Rand Road
Lake Zurich, IL 60047
847-438-7603

INDIANA

**Bridal Warehouse**
865 N. Green River Road
Evansville, IN 47715
812-471-9993
www.usabridal.com

**Bridal Warehouse**
705 E. Highway 31
Clarksville, IN 47129
812-288-8055
www.usabridal.com

**Carol's Bridal and Formal Wear**
110 Alpha & Omega Center
Charlestown Road & Hwy 60
Sellersburg, IN 47172
812-246-4220

**Formal Affairs**
23797 US 33
Elkhart, IN 46517
574-875-6654

**Greta's Bridal & Formalwear Shoppe**
1130 Lincoln Way East
South Bend, IN 46601
574-234-5777

**Posie Patch Bridal Superstores**
**Indy North**
8418 Castleton Corner Drive
Indianapolis North, IN 46250
317-849-9980
**Indy South**
5905 Madison Avenue
Indianapolis South, IN 46227
317-784-9980
www.posiepatchbridalsuperstores.com

KANSAS

**Audra's Ltd.**
2931 SW Topeka Boulevard
Topeka, KS 66611
785-266-7979

**Laura's Couture Collection**
13010 Shawnee Mission Parkway
Shawnee, KS 66216
913-631-3010
www.laurascouture.com

**Margie's Bridal & Tuxedo**
7421 West 91st Street
Overland Park, KS 66212
913-642-8108

**Parrot-Fa-Nalia**
1719 S. Hillside
Wichita, KS 67211
316-682-5531/800-669-3262

KENTUCKY

**Abbingtons**
1531 Frederica Street
Owensboro, KY 42301
270-684-4547

**Bridal Warehouse**
723 Hawkins Drive
Elizabethtown, KY 42701
270-737-3272
www.usabridal.com

**Bridal Warehouse**
1846 S. Hurstbourne Lane
Louisville, KY 40220
502-499-7911
www.usabridal.com

**Ruth's The Brides Shoppe**
153 Patchen Drive, Suite 51
Lexington, KY 40517
859-266-0754

LOUISIANA

**Bridal Boutique**
8750 Florida Boulevard
Baton Rouge, LA 70815
225-925-1135

**Pearl's Place**
3114 Severn Avenue
Metairie, LA 70002
504-885-9213

MAINE

**Patricia Buck Bridal**
275 Water Street
Augusta, ME 04330
207-622-6224
www.weddingwear.com

MARYLAND

**Betsy Robinson's Bridal Collection**
1848 Reisterstown Road
Baltimore, MD 21208
410-484-4600
www.robinsonsbridal.com

**Marlene's Bridal**
10130 Southern Maryland Boulevard
Dunkirk, MD 20754
301-855-7170

**Martins Bridal & Formal Shop**
1583 Sulphur Spring Road
Baltimore, MD 21227
410-595-0130
www.members.aol.com/baltbride

**Wedding Day by Design &
Perfect Fit Tuxedos**
6490 Dobbin Road
Columbia, MD 21045
410-884-0038

**Wedding Day by Design & Perfect Fit
Tuxedos**
7900 Ritchie Highway
Glen Burnie, MD 21061
410-761-6776
www.members.aol.com/baltbride

**Wedding Day by Design & Perfect Fit
Tuxedos**
5241 Buckeystown Pike
Frederick, MD 21703
301-688-9800

MASSACHUSETTS

**Alexandra's Boutique**
452 S. Main Street
Fall River, MA 02721
508-679-8770

**Bridal and Gift at Shear Style**
9 Washington Street, Route 1
Attleboro, MA 02703
508-399-6040
www.bridalandgift.com

**New York Lace**
89 Main Street
Taunton, MA 02790
508-824-6900

**Yolanda Enterprises, Inc.**
355 Waverly Oaks Road
Waltham, MA 02452
781-899-6470
www.yolandas.com

MICHIGAN

**Alvin's Bride**
26717 Little Mack Avenue
St. Clair Shores, MI 48081
586-498-7200

**"I Do" Too! Bridal**
345 North Main
Plymouth, MI 48170
734-455-4800
www.IDoTooBridal.com

**Julie Bridal Import**
34000 South Woodward Avenue
Birmingham, MI 48009
248-645-0500

**Lett's Bridal & Fashions**
1615 E. Michigan Avenue
Lansing, MI 48912
517-484-5359
www.lettsbridal.com

MINNESOTA

**Bridal Center**
7166 N. 10th Street
Oakdale, MN 55128
www.ibridalcenter.com

**Bridal Center**
4416 Lancaster Lane
Plymouth, MN 55441
763-550-3992
www.ibridalcenter.com

**The Hope Chest**
142 N. Buchanan Street, Suite 142
Cambridge, MN 55008
800-350-5482
www.thehopechestbridal.com

**Marshall Field's**
700 On the Mall
Minneapolis, MN 55402
612-375-2596
www.marshallfields.com

**Mestad's Bridal & Formalwear**
**Store #15101**
1171 6th Street NW
Rochester, MN 55901
507-289-2444
800-294-2440
**Store #15105**
2940 West Division Street
St. Cloud, MN 56301
320-252-9634
888-695-5813
www.mestads.com

**North Country Bridal, Inc.**
830 S. Lake Street
Forest Lake, MN 55025
651-464-8222

**The Wedding Shoppe, Inc.**
1196 Grand Avenue
St Paul, MN 55105
612-298-1144
www.weddingshoppeinc.com

**Imagi-nations**
131 West Cherokee Street
Brookhaven, MS 39601
800-676-1093
601-833-6280
www.imagi-nations.com

**The Bridal Path**
4465 I55 North Banner Hall
Suite 104
Jackson, MS 39206
601-982-8267
www.bridalpathinc.com

MISSOURI

**Bridal Inspirations, Ltd.**
8448 Watson Road
St. Louis, MO 63119
314-849-1101
www.bridalinspirations.com

**The Ultimate Bride**
1512 S. Brentwood Boulevard
St. Louis, MO 63144
314-961-9997
www.theultimatebride.com

NORTH CAROLINA

**Brennan's Bridal, Prom and Tux**
1606 South Stratford Road
Winston Salem, NC 27103
336-659-1233
www.brennansbridal.com

**Bridal Mart**
2450 Corporation Parkway
Burlington, NC 27215
336-227-5500
www.bridalmart.com

**Carolina Bridal World**
230 Venture Drive
Smithfield, NC 27577
877-274-3372
www.carolinabridalworld.com

**Enchanting Moments, Inc.**
132 South Fuquay Avenue
Fuquay-Varina, NC 27526
910-552-6393

**Kristy Lynn Bridals**
3121 N. Sharon Amity Road
Charlotte, NC 28205
704-531-8985
www.kristylynnbridals.com

**Mecklenburg Bridal Gallery**
8418-C Park Road
Charlotte, NC 28210
704-556-7789
www.mecklenburgbridal.com

**Mordecai Bridal and Tuxedo, Inc.**
707-09 Person Street
Raleigh, NC 27604
919-832-6447

**Western Carolina's Wedding Center**
85 Tunnel Road, Suite 29
Asheville, NC 28805
828-281-1532

NEVADA

**Bridal & Etc.**
4480 Spring Mountain Road, #400
Las Vegas, NV 89102
702-893-9770
www.bridaletc.com

**Celebration Bridal**
3131 South Jones Boulevard
Las Vegas, NV 89146
702-220-0507

NEW HAMPSHIRE

**Country Bridals & Formal Wear**
9 Blake Street
Jaffrey, NH 03452
603-532-7641
www.countrybridals.com

**Madeleine's Daughter Bridal**
100 Spaulding Turnpike
Portsmouth, NH 03801
603-431-5454
www.madeleinesdaughter.com

**Marry and Tux Shoppe**
100 Daniel Webster Highway
Nashua, NH 03060
603-883-6999

NEW JERSEY

**Bridal Suite of Ridgewood**
216 E. Ridgewood Avenue
Ridgewood, NJ 07450
201-444-3560

**Bridal Garden**
900 West Route 70
Marlton, NJ 08053
856-988-8188

**Bridals by Michelle Renee**
1415 Chambers Street
Trenton, NJ 08610
609-989-8185

**Reba's**
7111 Bergenline Avenue
North Bergen, NJ 07047
201-869-7172

NEW YORK

**Allisa's Bridal**
886 East 59th Street
Brooklyn, NY 11234
718-531-0608

**Amsale**
625 Madison Avenue
New York, NY 10022
212-583-1700
www.amsalewoman.net

**Bridal Hall**
2544 Ridgeway Avenue
Rochester, NY 14626-4116
585-225-3500

**Bridal Reflections**
80 Westbury Avenue
Carle Place, NY 15514
516-742-7788
3 Broadway
Massapequa, NY 11758
516-795-2222
www.bridalreflections.com

**Bridal Suite of Bay Shore**
7 East Main Street
Bay Shore, NY 11706
516-666-0700

**The Bridal Suite of Manhattan**
262 West 38th Street, 17th Floor
New York, New York 10018
212-764-3040
www.bridalsuitenyc.com

**Flowerama's Bridal Plaza**
59-35 Myrtle Avenue
Glendale, New York 11385
718-366-9656
1444 Hempstead Turnpike
Elmont, New York 11003
516-775-0489

**Fontana Bridal Salon**
678 White Plains Road
Scarsdale, NY 10583
914-472-1441
www.fontanabridalsalon.com

**House of Botticelli**
40 Pondfield Road
Bronxville, NY 10708
914-337-6384
www.houseofbotticelli.com

**Kleinfeld Bridal**
8202 5th Avenue
Brooklyn, NY 11209
718-765-8500
www.kleinfeldbridal.com

**Cillette's Bridals**
861 Merrick Road
Baldwin, NY 11510
516-546-5660

**R.K. Bridal**
318 West 39th Street
New York, NY 10018
212-947-1155/800-929-9512
www.rkbridal.com

**Vera Wang**
991 Madison Avenue
New York, NY 10022
212-628-3400
www.verawang.com

OHIO

**Bridal & Formal, Inc.**
300 W. Benson Street
Cincinnati, OH 45215
513-821-6622
www.bridalandformalinc.com

**Brides by Donna**
49 W. Orange Street
Chagrin Falls, OH 44022
440-247-1100

**Catan's Southern Plantation**
12878 Pearl Road
Strongsville, OH 44136
440-238-6664
www.catanbridal.com

**Henri's Cloud Nine**
110 N. Market Street
Minerva, OH 44657
330-868-6160/800-952-3560
www.henris.com

**House of Hilton**
2234 North Reynolds Road
Toledo, OH 43615
419-535-0661
www.houseofhilton.com

**Universe "The Ultimate Bridal Superstore"**
56310 US 36
West Lafayette, OH 43845
740-545-5005
www.ohiobride.net

**Laura Salkin**
20235 Van Aken Boulevard
Van Aken Shopping Center
Shaker Heights, OH 44122
216-921-2500

**Matina's**
28480 Chagrin Boulevard
Woodmere, OH 44122
216-464-1288

OKLAHOMA

**Besharás Formal Wear**
1660 E. 71st Street
Tulsa, OK 74136
918-492-4100

**J. J. Kelly Bridal Salon**
12325 North May Avenue
Oklahoma City, OK 73120
405-752-0029
www.jjkellybridal.com

OREGON

**Angela's Bridal Mart and Factory Outlet of Oregon**
788 S. Front Street
Central Point, OR 97502
541-665-6999
www.abridal.com

**Bridal Exclusives**
8950 Sunnyside Road
Clackamas, OR 97015
503-659-3766

**Dee's Studio, Ltd.**
20 NW Third
Gresham, OR 97030
503-665-4666
www.deesstudio.com

**Tower Bridal**
5331 SW Macadam Avenue, #128
Portland, OR 97405
503-274-8940
www.towerbridal.com

**Tres Fabu Bridal**
6910 SE Milwaukee Avenue
Portland, OR 97266
503-233-0004

PENNSYLVANIA
**Anne Bailey's**
4975 Swamp Road
Fountainville, PA 18923
215-345-8133
www.annebaileys.com

**Bliss Brides**
37 South Courtland Street
East Stroudsburg, PA 18301
570-426-3180

**Bridaltown**
3446 Germantown Pike
Collegeville, PA 19426
610-489-1950
www.bridaltown.net

**Carlisle's of Pittsburgh**
2549 Penn Avenue
Pittsburgh, PA 15222
412-321-2421
www.bridalwear.com

**Formalities by Tracina Fisher**
121 South Alleghany Street
Bellefonte, PA 16823
814-357-2060

**Simone's Unlimited Bridal &
Day Spa**
332 East Middle Street
Hanover, PA 17331
717-630-0990
www.simonesunlimited.com

**Suky Rosan**
102 East Montgomery Avenue
Ardmore, PA 19003
610-649-3686
www.sukyrosan.com

SOUTH CAROLINA
**A Wedding Place**
26 Aberdeen Drive
Greenville, SC 29605
864-271-0516

**Dimitra Mandala Designs**
730 S. Pleasantburg Drive
Greenville, SC 29607
864-467-0801
www.dimitradesigns.com

**Special Occasions & Such**
218 Commerce Street
Manning, SC 29102
803-435-0733

**The White Room**
706 East Washington Street
Greenville, SC 29601
864-232-5778

TENNESSEE
**Arzelle's**
2926 W. End Avenue
Nashville, TN 37203
615-327-1020

**Bridal Gallery and Chapel**
4247 South Carothers Road
Franklin, TN 37067
615-794-1398
www.bridalgallery.citysearch.com

**Bridal Warehouse**
900 Conference Drive
Goodlettsville, TN 37072
615-855-1005
www.usabridal.com

**Lillian's Bridal**
201 College Street
Gleason, TN 38229
731-648-1444

**Monica's**
147 North Market Street
Chattanooga, TN 37405
423-752-0072
www.monicasbridal.com

**White Lace and Promises**
10001 Kingston Pike
Knoxville, TN 37922
865-693-9399

TEXAS

**Brickhouse Bridal**
200 Valleywood Street, Suite A-30
The Woodlands, TX 77380
281-681-3430
www.brickhousebridal.com

**Bridal Galleria**
3801 San Bernardo Street
Laredo, TX 78041
956-791-9567

**The Bridal Portfolio**
104 N. Tennessee
Mckinney, TX 75069
972-562-9779

**Bridesave.com**
Courtyard at Midland Park
4410 North Midkiff Road
Midland, TX 79705
888-321-4696
www.bridesave.com

**Bridesmart**
7807 South Main
Houston, TX 77030
713-791-1888
www.bridesmart.com

**Elodia Boutique & Bridal**
1331 N. Lee Trevino Drive
El Paso, TX 79936
915-595-1997

**Louise Blum Couture Bridal**
1801 Post Oak Boulevard
Houston, TX 77056
713-791-1888
www.louiseblum.com

**Mockingbird Bridal**
5602 East Mockingbird Lane
Dallas, TX 75206
214-828-5616
www.mockingbirdbridal.com

**Neiman Marcus**
400 Northpark Center
Dallas, TX 75225
214-363-8311
www.meimanmarcus.com

**Ocones**
6333 Camp Bowie Boulevard
Fort Worth, TX 76116
817-732-4457

UTAH

**Mary's Bridal**
6267 S. Highland Drive
Salt Lake City, UT 84121
801-278-7106

**Seven Oaks Bridal**
6775 South 900 East
Salt Lake City, UT 84047
801-566-1100
www.70aksreceptions.com

VIRGINIA

**Eileen Originals Formal & Bridal**
5386 Kemps River Drive, Suite 111
Virginia Beach, VA 23464
757-424-0107

**Hannelore's**
423 King Street
Alexandria, VA 22314
703-369-1998
www.hannelores.com

**Jeanette's Bride N Tuxedo Boutique**
10386 Festival Lane
Manassas, VA 20109
703-369-1998

**Karen Eagle**
11114 West Broad Street
Glen Allen, VA 23060
804-360-8120
www.kareneagle.com

**Tiffanys**
12 Best Square
Norfolk, VA 23502
757-461-1690
www.tiffanysbridal.com

**Rosalin's Bridal Boutique**
706 South Washington Street
Falls Church, VA 22046
703-532-0288
www.rosalinsbridal.com

WASHINGTON, D.C.
**Rizik Bros**
1100 Connecticut Avenue NW
Washington, D.C. 20036
202-223-4050

WASHINGTON
**Bridal Collections**
120 North Stevens
Spokane, WA 99201
509-838-1210
www.thebridalcollections.com

**Marcella's La Boutique**
1417 4th Avenue, #200
Seattle, WA 98101
206-264-0792

**The Bridal Garden**
10 Lakeshore Plaza
Kirkland, WA 98033
425-889-2151
www.thebridalgarden.com

WISCONSIN
**Edith's of Fond du Lac**
PO Box 1336
9 South Main Street
Fond du Lac, WI 54936
920-921-2420
www.ediths.com

**Elaine's House of Brides**
906 Hansen Road
Green Bay, WI 54304
920-498-8998
www.elaineshouseofbrides.com

**GiGi of Mequon**
1550 Mequon Road
Mequon, WI 53092
262-241-1123
www.gigiofmequon.com

**Mestad's Bridal & Formalwear**
Store #15113
2713 N. Claremont Avenue
Westridge Center
Eau Claire, WI 54703
715-834-7744
www.mestads.com

**Nedrebo's Bridal**
4522 E. Washington Avenue
Madison, WI 53704
608-246-2800
www.nedrebos.com

**Nedrebo's Bridal**
5237 Verona Road
Madison, WI 53717
608-271-1042
www.nedrebos.com

**Nedrebo's Bridal**
601 Junction Road
Madison, WI 53711
608-833-4995
www.nedrebos.com

WEST VIRGINIA
**Harvey's Fashion & Bridal**
104 Beckley Plaza Mall
Beckley, WV 25801
304-253-2055

**Kaufman's, Inc.**
1040 Main Street
Wheeling, WV 26003
304-233-2309

## WEDDING GOWNS AND ACCESSORIES

### KEY
BM=BRIDESMAID
FG=FLOWER GIRL
HP=HEADPIECES
MOB=MOTHER OF THE BRIDE
SO=SOCIAL OCCASION
WG=WEDDING GOWNS

**AA Bridal**
4115 Schaefer Avenue
Chino, CA 91710
800-873-1355
HP, Veils

**Acconciature Carla/Di Carla Ragaini**
**Via Luigi Francesconi**
Tolentino, Italy 62029
39-07-339-73122
www.carla.it
HP, Veils, Gloves

**Adele Wechsler**
1912 Avenue Road
Toronto, Ontario, Canada M5M 4A1
416-787-5768
www.adelewechsler.com
WG

**Adrianna Papell, LLC**
498 Seventh Avenue, 6th Floor
New York, NY 10018
212-695-5244
MOB

**Affinité Collection**
89 Tycos Drive, Suite 100
Toronto, Ontario, Canada M6B 1W3
416-504-9600
www.affinitebridals.com
WG

**After Dark by**
**Mark Henry Fashions, Inc.**
640 West Street Road
Feasterville, PA 19053
215-357-1815
www.internetbridalmarket.com/
markhenry.htm
MOB, SO

**Aimee Monet Formal Fashion**
PO Box 880596
San Diego, CA 92168
800-313-8768
www.lastmem.com
BM, FG

**Alex Evenings**
1400 Broadway, 20th Floor
New York, NY 10018
800-ALEX-EVE
www.alexevenings.com
MOB, SO

**Alex Hanson Bridal**
3410 Midland Avenue, Unit 1
Toronto, Ontario, Canada M1V 4V4
416-292-7614
www.alexhansonbridal.com
WG, BM, SO

**Aleya Bridal**
265 W. Patrick Street
Frederick, MD 21701
301-631-6558
www.aleya.com
WG

**Alfred Angelo**
116 Welsh Road
Horsham, PA 19044
800-531-1125
www.alfredangelo.com
WG, BM, MOB, SO, HP, Veils

**Alfred Sung Bridals**
15 Ingram Drive
Toronto, Ontario, Canada M6M 2L7
989-275-2100
www.alfredsungbridals.com
WG

**Alfred Sung Bridesmaids/Algo**
5555 Cypihot Street
Saint-Laurent, Quebec
Canada H45 1R3
800-295-7308
www.loriann.com
BM, MOB, SO

**Allegro**
PO Box 1243
Pasadena, MD 21123
410-255-7114
HP, Veils

**Allin Rae**
275 Danforth Avenue
Toronto, Ontario, Canada M4K 1N4
416-469-1098
WG, HP, Veils

**Allure**
7601 Highway 64
Memphis, TN 38133
901-385-1400
www.allurebridals.com
WG

**Alvina Valenta**
501 Seventh Avenue, Suite 1318
New York, NY 10018
212-354-6798
www.alvinavalenta.com
WG

**Alyce Designs**
7901 North Caldwell
Morton Grove, IL 60053
800-775-2592
www.alycedesigns.com
BM, MOB, SO

**Amalia Carrara**
1375 Broadway, 7th Floor
New York, NY 10018
201-553-9799
WG

**Amsale**
347 W. 39th Street, Suite 11N
New York, NY 10018
800-765-0170
www.amsale.com
WG, BM

**Amy Kuschel Bride**
1933 Davis Street, Suite 232
San Leandro, CA 94577
510-632-2807
www.amykuschel.com
WG

**Amy Lee by Hilton Bridal**
3905 Braxton Drive
Houston, TX 77063
800-399-6353
www.amyleebridal.com
WG, BM, MOB

**Amy Michelson**
12198 Ventura Boulevard, #103
Studio City, CA 91604
818-755-1599
www.amymichelson.com
WG, HP, Veils

**Angel Sanchez**
526 Seventh Avenue, 9th Floor
New York, NY 10018
212-921-9827
www.angelsanchez.com
WG

**Angelina Bridal Couture**
120 Fonston Street
Hollywood, FL 33019
305-812-4968
WG

**Anjolique Bridal Collection**
230 Regina Street N.
Waterloo, Ontario, Canada N2J 3B6
519-725-2588
www.anjolique.com
WG

**Anna Chung**
310 High Street
Monterey, CA 93940
415-250-0387
www.annachung.com
WG

**Anne Barge**
75 14th Street NE, Suite 2701
Atlanta, GA 30309
404-873-8070
www.annebarge.com
WG

**Ansonia Bridal Veils**
1416 Willow Avenue
Hoboken, NJ 07030
800-517-7222
www.ansoniabridal.com
HP, Veils

**Antonio Fermin Bridal Designs**
12536 Craig Street
Grandview, MO 64030
913-967-6779
WG

**Atelier Aimee**
831 Loring Street
San Diego, CA 92109
619-602-7318
WG

**August Veils**
2808 NE Martin Luther King Jr. Boulevard
Portland, OR 97212
503-788-5280
www.augustveils.com
HP, Veils

**Aurora D'Paradiso**
29295 Bryan Way
Punta Gorda, FL 33982
941-637-4947
www.formalsource.com
WG Plus Size

**Avanti Designs**
6015 Obispo Avenue
Long Beach, CA 90805
800-654-7375
MOB, SO

**Bari-Jay Bridesmaids**
225 W. 37th Street, 17th Floor
New York, NY 10018
212-921-1551
www.barijay.com
BM, MOB, SO

**Bayje**
7975 Soquel Drive
Aptos, CA 95003
800-942-7837
Accessories

**Bel Aire Bridal Veils**
23002 Mariposa Avenue
Torrance, CA 90502
800-992-9225
www.belaireveils.com
HP, Veils

**Bella Jane Sposa**
1222 East Boulevard
Charlotte, NC 28203
704-372-8573
www.bridesheadonline.com
Shoes, HP, Veils

**Belle of the Ball**
4250 Encinas Drive
La Canada, CA 91011
818-952-8111
www.belleoftheball.net
FG

**Benjamin Walk Corporation**
PO Box 627, 511 Route 125
Barrington, NH 03825
800-621-0029
www.touchups.com
Shoes

Betty Wales Bridal Veils
135 W. 36th Street, 17th Floor
New York, NY 10018
888-777-VEIL
www.bettywales.com
HP, Veils

**Beverly Clark Collection**
1750 S. Waukegan Road
Waukegan, IL 60085
847-887-0071
www.beverlyclark.com
Accessories

**Bill Levkoff**
29-09 37th Avenue
Long Island City, NY 11101
718-433-0027
www.billlevkoff.com
BM

**Birnbaum & Bullock**
27 W. 20th Street, # 703
New York, NY 10011
212-242-2914
www.birnbaumandbullock.com
WG, HP, Veils

**Blueberries**
7401 Fourth Avenue, #D10
Bayridge, NY 11209
917-273-9478
FG

**Bob Mackie Boutique**
530 Seventh Avenue, 3rd Floor
New York, NY 10018
212-719-0056
BM, MOB, SO

**Bolo Vasquez Bridal**
237 W. 35th Street, Suite 301
New York, NY 10001
212-760-2450
WG

**Bonny MT Enterprises**
2675 Saturn Street
Brea, CA 92821
800-528-0030
www.bonny.com
WG, HP, Veils

**Bouchard Wedding Collection**
612 W. Fifth Avenue
Naperville, IL 60563
800-967-5467
www.bouchardltd.com
Accessories

**The Bridal Garden**
10 Lake Shore Plaza
425-889-2151
Kirkland, WA 98033
www.thebridalgarden.com
WG

**Bridal Originals**
1700 St. Louis Road
Collinsville, IL 62234
618-345-4499
www.bridaloriginals.com
WG, BM, MOB, SO, HP, Veils

**Bridal Potpourri, Inc.**
39 W. 37th Street, 16th Floor
New York, NY 10018
800-666-4568
Accessories

**The Bridal Veil Company**
235 St. Marks Avenue
Brooklyn, NY 11238
718-623-0900
HP, Veils

**Bridals by Justine**
11940 Goldring Road, Unit B
Arcadia, CA 91006
800-866-4696
www.fleurdelisbyjustine.com
WG, FG, SO

**Cachet, Inc.**
1400 Broadway, 4th Floor
New York, NY 10018
212-398-1186
BM, MOB, SO

**Cait Couture**
21 Sawyer Road, Suite 100
North Andover, MA 01845
978-258-6142
www.caitcouture.com
HP, Veils, Accessories

**Cantu & Castillo Couture**
7415 Beverly Boulevard
Los Angeles, CA 90036
323-931-8325
www.cantucastillo.com
WG, SO

**Carmela Sutera, Inc.**
93 S. Main Street
Lodi, NJ 07644
973-471-7444
www.carmelasutera.com
WG

**Carol Lambuth Couture**
2515 Berndatte Square
Columbia, MO 65203
573-445-7883
WG, BM, FG, MOB, SO

**Carol Peretz**
121 Lakeville Road
New Hyde Park, NY 11040
516-328-7271
MOB, SO

**Carolina Amato Glove Collection**
15 W. 37th Street, 8th Floor
New York, NY 10018
212-768-9095
www.carolinaamato.com
HP, Veils, Gloves, Accessories

**Carolina Herrerra**
501 7th Avenue
New York, NY 10018
212-944-5757
www.carolinaherrrera.com
WG

**Casablanca**
760 Debra Lane
Anaheim, CA 92805
714-758-8888
www.casablancabridal.com
WG

**Cassandra Stone by Creative Imports**
4650 Western Avenue
Lisle, IL 60532
630-663-1000
www.cassandrastone.com
MOB, SO

**Caterina Collection**
1385 Broadway, 20th Floor
New York, NY 10018
212-921-5560
www.jordanfashions.com
MOB, SO

**Catherine Regehr**
111-159 W. 6th Avenue
Vancouver, BC, Canada B6J 1R1
604-734-9339
WG, MOB, BM

**Charo Peres, Inc.**
2061 Wright Avenue, Suite A-5
La Verne, CA 91750
909-596-2220
www.charoperes.com
WG

**Che Bella**
308 Prince Street, Studio 234
St. Paul, MN 55101
651-292-1618
www.chebella.com
HP, Veils

**Christina Wu**
14975 Technology Court
Ft. Myers, FL 33912
239-277-7099
www.christinawu.net
WG

**Christos, Inc.**
241 W. 37th Street, 6th Floor
New York, NY 10018
212-921-0025
www.christosbridal.com
WG

**Clea Colet**
260 W. 39th Street, 17th Floor
New York, NY 10018
212-382-2437
www.cleacolet.com
WG

**Cocoe Voci**
185 N. Robertson Boulevard
Beverly Hills, CA 90211
310-360-0287
www.cocoevoci.com
WG

**Coloriffics**
Speen & Company, Inc.
PO Box 2408
Woburn, MA 1888
800-225-5746
www.coloriffics.com
Shoes

**Cristina Arzuaga & Co., Inc.**
200 East 15th Street
New York, NY 10011
212-780-9647
WG

**Cynthia C. & Co.**
360 Mount Pleasant Road
Mamaroneck, NY 10543
914-777-6648
WG

**Damianou**
32-01 57th Street
Woodside, NY 11377
718-204-5600
MOB, SO

**Daymour U.S.A., LLC**
602 Neponset Street
Canton, MA 02021
781-821-1270
www.daymor.com
MOB, SO

**Demetrios**
222 W. 37th Street
New York, NY 10018
212-967-5222
www.demetriosbride.com
WG

**Dere Kiang**
14975 Technology Court
Ft. Myers, FL 33912
239-277-7099
www.derekiang.com
WG

**The Dessy Group**
118 West 20th Street
New York, NY 10011
646-638-9600
www.thedessygroup.com
WG, BM, SO

**Domo Adami**
39-038-182-100
www.domoadami.com
WG

**Donna Salado**
819 Lee Street
Charleston, WV 25301
304-346-9016
WG

**Dyeables**
PO Box 90
16 Mt. Ebo Road
S. Brewster, NY 10509
800-431-2000
www.dyeables.com
Shoes

**Eden Bridals**
145 E. Walnut Avenue
Monrovia, CA 91016
626-358-9281
www.edenbridals.com
WG, BM

**Edgardo Bonilla Bridal Collection**
300 Kings Highway E., Suite 11
Haddonfield, NJ 08033
856-216-7726x2
WG

**Edward E. Berger**
148 W. 37th Street, 7th Floor
New York, NY 10018
212-594-0400
www.edwardberger.com
Shoes

**Eliana Ben-Zeev**
1123 N. Flores Street, Suite 17
Hollywood, CA 90069
323-848-8844
WG, MOB, SO

**Elizabeth Fillmore**
130 W. 23rd Street
New York, NY 10011
212-647-0863
WG

**Emanuelle**
1375 Broadway
New York, NY 10018
212-302-0050
WG

**Eponymo Bridal, Inc.**
2401 Ingleside Avenue, Unit 8C
Cincinnati, OH 45206
513-961-8029
WG, HP, Veils

**Erica Koesler Wedding Accessories**
12142 Sherman Way
N. Hollywood, CA 91605
818-764-1913
www.ericakoesler.com
HP, Veils

**Erin Cole Design**
1725 Monrovia Avenue, #B-1
Costa Mesa, CA 92627
949-642-8646
www.erincole.com
HP, Veils, Accessories

**Etienne Bresson**
6634 Leland Way
Los Angeles, CA 90028
323-464-7500
www.etiennebresson.com
FG

**Eugenia**
83 West Broad Street
Bethleham, PA 18018
610-866-5181
www.eugeniacouture.com
WG

**Everbeauty**
400 Broadway, 3rd Floor
New York, NY 10018
212-997-1919
www.everbeauty.com
MOB, BM, SO

**Fashion 1001 Nights/Nina Canacci**
3025 S. Figueroa Street
Los Angeles, CA 90007
800-919-1001
www.fashion1001nights.com
MOB, BM, SO

**Faviana**
70 W. 36th Street
New York, NY 10018
800-2-FAVANIA
www.faviana.com
WG, BM, SO

**Fenaroli for Regalia**
281 Summer Street, 4th Floor
Boston, MA 02210
617-723-3682
www.fenaroli.com
HP, Veils, Accessories

**Finale Gloves**
375 Pearsall Avenue
Cedarhurst, NY 11516
516-371-1313
www.finalegloves.com
Gloves

**Forsyth Enterprises**
25 Seabreeze Avenue
Delray Beach, FL 32483
561-244-0400
WG

**Frederico Leone by Colonial Shoe**
PO Box 43001
Atlanta, GA 30336
800-678-7463
Shoes

**Gabalis**
526 Seventh Avenue, 6th Floor
New York, NY 10018
212-921-1099
MOB, SO

**Germar Exclusivas**
Parroquia 829-1
Col. De Valle, Mexico D.F. 3100
212-877-5836
www.martalomelin.com
WG

**Giavan**
191 Rampo Valley Road
Oakland, NJ 07436
800-344-2826
HP

**Giovanna Sbiroli**
SS 37 x Castellana Grotte
Putignano (BA), Italy 70017
39-080-4977400
www.giovannasbiroli.it
WG

**Glatter & Sims**
1375 Broadway, 10th Floor
New York, NY 10018
212-391-0150
www.internetbridalmarket.com/glatter.htm
MOB, SO

**Golden Gate Bridal**
805 Secretary Drive, Suite E
Arlington, TX 76015
800-233-9919
www.goldengatebridal.com
WG, FG

**Gordon Couture**
2300 Dixie Road
Mississauga, Ontario, Canada
LY4 1Z4
905-276-3399
www.gordonbrides.com
WG, MOB, SO

**Guzzo**
30 Duncan Street
Toronto, Ontario,
Canada M5V 2C3
416-585-9820
www.guzzo-bridal.com
WG

**Halo & Co. International**
205 E. 22nd Street, #5
New York, NY 10010
212-696-2318
www.haloandco.com
Accessories

**Headpieces by Toni**
108 N. 10th Street
Mount Vernon, NY 62864
618-244-4842
HP, Veils

**Helen Morley Bride**
226 W. 37th Street, 4th Floor
New York, NY 10018
212-594-6104
www.helenmorley.com
WG, SO

**Homa Creations**
27 Main Street
Millburn, NJ 07041
973-467-5500
HP, Veils, Accessories

**Ian Stuart International**
360 Route 59
Airmont, NY 10952
845-369-6631
www.ianstuart.com
WG

**Illusions Bridal**
859 East Grand Avenue
Fruita, CO 81521
800-443-9102
www.illusionsbridal.com
HP, Veils

**Impression Bridal**
501 FM 1092
Stafford, TX 77477
800-BRIDAL-1
www.impressionbridal.com
WG, BM

**Ines Di Santo Corp.**
90 Winges Avenue W, Unit 14
Woodbridge, Ontario
Canada L4L 6Y6
905-856-9115
www.inesdisanto.com
WG, MOB, SO

**Ivonne De La Vega Couture**
66 NW 22nd Avenue
Miami, FL 33125
305-631-0633
www.ivonnedelavega.com
WG, SO

**Jacqueline Bridals**
14975 Technology Court
Ft. Myers, FL 33912
239-277-7099
www.jacquelinbridals.com
WG

**Janell Berte**
248 East Liberty Street
Lancaster, PA 17602
717-291-9894
www.berte.com
WG, BM, HP, Veils

**Janet Nelson Kumar**
245 Bennett Avenue, #2A
New York, NY 10040
212-942-1161
www.janetnelsonkumar.com
WG

**Jasmine**
820 Turnberry Court
Hanover Park, IL 60133
800-634-0224
www.jasminebridal.com
WG, BM

**Jasz Formals**
1143 S. Los Angeles Street
Los Angeles, CA 90015
213-744-1842
MOB, SO

**Je Matadi Dress Co. Inc.**
PO Box 710624
Houston, TX 77271
888-839-1293
www.jematadi.com
MOB, SO

**Jennifer Leigh**
1200 Harris Avenue, #411
Bellingham, WA 98225
360-714-0992
www.jenniferleigh.com
HP, Veils

**Jenny Lee Bridal**
422 N. La Genga Boulevard
2nd Floor
Los Angeles, CA 90041
310-652-9293
www.jennyleebridal.com
WG

**Jessica Lynn**
61 Hays Drive
Blountsville, AL 35031
800-242-1092
FG, SO, HP, Veils

**Jessica McClintock**
1400 16th Street
San Francisco, CA 94103
800-333-5301
www.jessicamcclintock.com
WG, BM, MOB, SO, FG, HP, Veils

**Jim Hjelm Couture**
525 Seventh Avenue
New York, NY 10018
212-764-6960
www.jimhjelm.com
WG, BM

**Joan Calabrese**
1101 Sussex Boulevard, Lower Level
Broomall, PA 19008
610-604-0900
www.joancalabrese.net
FG

**John Russell**
1444 Oaklawn Avenue, Suite 200
Dallas, TX 75207
214-528-1975
www.johnrussellapparel.com
WG, MOB, SO

**Jordan Fashion**
1385 Broadway, 20th Floor
New York, NY 10018
212-921-5560
www.jordanfashions.com
MOB, SO, FG

**Joseph Reynolds Couture**
PO Box 78986
Atlanta, GA 30357
404-603-8280
WG, SO

**Jovani Fashions**
498 Seventh Avenue, 15th Floor
New York, NY 10018
800-6-JOVANI
www.jovani.com
WG, MOB, SO

**JS Group**
1400 Broadway, #702
New York, NY 10018
212-354-4700
MOB, SO

**Justina McCaffrey**
10 Amherst Street
Quebec, Canada J8Y 6W1
888-874-GOWN
www.justinamccaffrey.com
WG, HP, Veils

**Kathryn & Alexandra**
2411 Kiesel Avenue, Suite 314
Ogden, UT 84401
801-392-8382
www.kathrynandalexandra.com
WG, SO, FG

**Kay Bingham**
6200 SW 79th Court
Miami, FL 33143
877-712-4361
www.kaybingham.com
Accessories

**Kelly Chase**
105 Valley View Road
Mount Horeb, WI 53572
608-437-1983
www.kellychase.com
WG

**Kenneth Cole**
152 West 57th Street, 15th Floor
New York, NY 10019
212-265-1500
www.kennethcole.com
Shoes

**Kristina Eaton, LTD**
4112 Mulligan Lane
Acworth, GA 30101
800-321-VEIL
www.kristinaeatonltd.com
HP, Veils, Accessories

**La Sposa**
55 Johnson Road
Lawrence, NY 11559
888-776-6684
www.splasposa.com
WG, Accessories

**Labelle Fashions**
14975 Technology Court
Ft. Meyers, FL 33912
239-277-7099
www.labellefashions.net
MOB, SO

**Lady Roi Bridals**
460 Main Avenue
Wallington, NJ 07057
888-802-8588
www.ladyroibridals.com
WG

**L'Amour Bridal, Inc.**
14662 Franklin Avenue, Unit G
Tustin, CA 92870
714-838-5683
www.lamourbridals.com
WG, BM, HP, Veils

**Landa Designs**
106 Schelter Road
Lincolnshire, IL 60069
800-366-8168
www.landadesigns.com
WG, BM, SO

**Le Stella**
4961 Santa Anita Avenue, Suite G
Temple City, CA 91780
888-626-7888
www.lestella.com
WG, BM, FG

**Le Spose di Carmen**
Via Lucania 54
Ginosa (TA), Italy 74013
39-99-821-5719
www.lesposedicarmen.com
WG

**Lebon Bridal**
20459 Valley Boulevard
Walnut, CA 91789
909-468-3777
www.lebonbridal.com
WG

**L'Ezu Atelier**
247 South Robertson Boulevard
Beverly Hills, CA 90211
310-657-5398
www.lezu.com
WG

**Lisa Gowing**
218 New South Head Road
Double Bay
Sydney, New South Wales, Australia
866-684-0658
www.lisagowing.com
WG

**Little Angels**
850 S. Broadway, Suite 1101
Los Angeles, CA 90014
213-624-4477
www.usangels.com
FG

**Lizette Creations, Inc.**
950 W. 12th Street
Long Beach, CA 90813
800-725-9458
www.lizettecreations.com
BM, SO

**Loralie**
5113 Commercial Drive
North Richmond Hills, TX 76180
817-605-9004
www.loralie.com
BM, SO

**Lori London**
5045 Franklin Avenue
Los Angeles, CA 90027
323-644-1109
www.lorilondon.com
BM, MOB, SO

**Love Illusions**
18 Stephens Street
Belleville, NJ 07109
973-844-0582
WG

**Lynn Litwin**
858 W. Armitage, #308
Chicago, IL 60614
773-281-3003
Accessories

**M & B Hairlooms**
360 Mount Pleasant Road
Mamaroneck, NY 10543
914-670-0377
HP, Veils, Accessories

**Macis, Inc.**
11 Harts Lane, Suite M
E. Brunswick, NJ 08816
732-698-9848
MOB, SO, FG

**Mackenzie Michaels**
2153 Pond Road
Ronkonkoma, NY 11779
631-285-7850
www.mackenziemichaels.com
BM

**Madison Collection**
2770 Dufferin Street, 2nd Floor
Toronto, Ontario, Canada M6B 3R7
416-789-9911
WG

**Maggie Sottero**
2300 S. 1070 W.
Salt Lake City, UT 84119
801-975-8138
www.maggiesotterobridal.com
WG

**Malis-Henderson, Inc.**
8255 Mountain Sights, Suite 101
Montreal, Canada H4P 2B5
514-344-2254
www.mhtiara.com
HP, Veils

**Manalé**
260 W. 39th Street, #1101
New York, NY 10018
212-944-6939
www.manale.com
WG, SO

**Marabella**
2204 W. Torrance Boulevard
Suite 101
Torrance, CA 90050
425-259-3900
WG

**Marcela Creations**
1802 W. Kennedy Road
Tampa, FL 33606
800-633-3097
www.marcelacreations.com
Accessories

**Maria Elena Headpieces**
Industrial Park
7931 NW 64th Street
Miami, FL 33166
305-717-3404
HP, Veils

**Mariell Designs**
98 Route 46
Budd Lake, NJ 07828
800-248-6264
www.mariellonline.com
Accessories

**Marisa**
501 Seventh Avenue, Suite 418
New York, NY 10018
212-944-0022
www.marisabridals.com
WG

**Maritza's Bridal Veils**
4471 SW 75th Avenue
305-263-6606
Miami, FL 33165
HP, Veils

**Martinez Valero**
152 W. 57th Street
New York, NY 10019
212-757-0800
www.martinezvalero.com
Shoes

**Mary's Bridal**
10520 Kinghurst Drive
Houston, TX 77099
281-933-9678
www.marysbridal.com
WG, BM, MOB, SO, FG, HP, Veils

**Matthew Christopher**
165 East 104th Street
New York, NY 10029
212-289-4454
www.matthewchristopher.com
WG

**Max Chaoul**
Rue Francois Dauthin
Lyon, France 69002
33-4-7848-9625
WG

**Melissa Sweet Bridal Collection**
1816 Briarwood Industrial Court, Suite D
Atlanta, GA 30329
404-633-4395
www.melissasweet.com
WG, BM

**Mera by Valerie Michelle**
9734 Lipari Circle
Cypress, CA 90630
714-826-8266
www.merabride.com
WG, HP, Veils

**Merry Fashion, Inc./Merrymax**
2550 Corporate Place, Suite C-109
Monterey Park, CA 91754
323-780-8188
WG, FG, SO

**Mia Callaway Couture Bridal**
2853 Oldknow Drive
Atlanta, GA 30318
404-794-5801
www.mcbridal.com
WG, HP, Veils

**Michael of Boston**
25 Waterman Avenue
Marshfield, MA 02050
781-834-5769
www.michaelofboston.com
WG

**Mika Inatome**
11 Worth Street, Suite 4B
New York, NY 10013
800-224-6286
www.mikainatome.com
WG

**Mikayla Designs**
SAA # 2-703 Corydon Avenue
Winnipeg, Canada R3M 0W4
888-391-0547
HP, Veils

**Mike Benet**
12215 Forestgate
Dallas, TX 75243
214-340-1592
www.mikebenet.com
SO

**Miri Designs**
501 Seventh Avenue, Suite 506
New York, NY 10018
212-869-3844
www.miridesignsinc.com
WG

**Modeca**
Corporate Center
812 Proctor Avenue
Ogdensburg, NY 13669
613-340-6727
www.modeca.com
WG

**Modern Classics, Inc.**
1579 Barclay Boulevard
877-388-3838
WG

**Mon Cheri Bridals**
1018 Whitehead Road Extension
Trenton, NJ 08638
609-530-1900
www.moncheribridals.com
WG, BM, MOB, SO, HP, Veils, FG

**Monique Bridal**
10505 E. Valley Boulevard, #338
El Monte, CA 91731
626-401-9910
www.moniquebridal.com
WG, SO

**Monique Lhuillier, Inc.**
3611 Hayden Avenue
Culver City, CA 90232
310-559-4599
www.moniquelhuillier.com
WG, SO

**Montique**
2580 Corporate Place, Suite F-105
Monterey Park, CA 91754
626-350-3232
www.montique.com
WG, FG

**Mony Bridal and Evening Wear, Inc.**
2272 Marconi Avenue
Sacramento, CA 95821
916-925-5356
www.mony.com.tw
WG, SO

**Moonlight**
1400 Wilkening Road
Schaumburg, IL 60173
847-884-7199
www.moonlightbridal.com
WG

**Mori Lee**
512 Seventh Avenue, 26th Floor
New York, NY 1001
212-840-5070
WG, BM

**Ms. Jillian**
13 E. 37th Street
New York, NY 10016
212-532-5258
www.msjillian.com
Junior BM

**Nancy Issler "A Bride's Collection"**
116 Welsh Road
Horsham, PA 19044
877-228-7701
WG

**New Image**
29-09 37th Avenue
Long Island City, NY 11101
718-433-0027
www.newimagebridesmaids.com
BM, SO

**Nu Mode Dress Company Limited**
5 St Regis Crescent N.
Toronto, Ontario, Canada MJ3 1N3
888-703-6633
BM, MOB, SO

**Occasions**
525 Seventh Avenue, Suite 1701A
New York, NY 10018
800-686-7880
www.jimhjelmoccasions.com
BM, SO

**Obsessions Couture**
89 Tycos Drive, Suite 100
Toronto, Ontario, Canada M6B 1W3
416-504-9600
www.obsessionscouture.com
MOB, SO

**Oscar de la Renta Bridal**
93 S. Main Street
Lodi, NJ 07644
212-947-1160
WG

**Palazzo Bridal Gowns**
2262 N. Clark Street
Chicago, IL 60614
773-665-4044
www.palazzobridal.com
WG

**Pallas Athena**
Lotus Orient Corporation
PO Box 280
San Gabriel, CA 91778
800-648-3687
www.lotusorient.com
WG

**Paloma Blanca**
4324 Glenside Drive
Reading, PA 19605
416-235-0585
www.palomablanca.com
WG

**Panoply**
PO Box 78986
Atlanta, GA 30357
404-603-8280
www.panoplydesign.com
BM, SO

**Paris**
1624 Knowlton Street
Cincinnati, OH 45223
513-542-8345
www.paristiaras.com
HP, Veils

**Paula Varsalona**
1375 Broadway, 14th Floor
New York, NY 10018
212-221-5600
www.paulavarsalona.com
WG, BM, FG, HP

**Pegeen**
PO Box 27
Ironia, NJ 07845
973-442-0799
www.pegeen.com
FG

**Pesavento Couture**
208 W. 29th Street, Suite 509
New York, NY 10001
212-629-3004
MOB, SO

**Petals International**
Shadwell House
280 Shadwell Lane
Leeds, England LS17 8AJ
44-1132-660388
HP, Veils, Accessories

**Peter Fox Shoes**
2652 Templeton Drive
Vancouver, BC, Canada V5N 4W3
604-253-7071
www.peterfox.com
Shoes

**Peter Langner**
viale Parioli
Rome, Italy 6300198
39-06807-228
www.peterlangner.com
WG, SO

**Precious Formals**
451 Landing Boulevard
League City, TX 77573
888-285-9150
www.preciousformals.com
WG, BM, MOB, SO

**Private Label by G**
6015 Obispo Avenue
Long Beach, CA 90805
800-654-7375
www.privatelabelbyg.com
WG

**Pronovias**
55 Johnson Road
Lawrence, NY 11559
888-776-6684
www.pronovias.com
WG

**R & M Bridal Accessories**
1147 E. Broadway, #72
Glendale, CA 91205
800-888-7916
www.rmbridal.com
HP, Veils

**Rahmanian Couture**
83 Yorkville Avenue
Toronto, Ontario, Canada M5R 1C1
800-380-1946
www.rahmanian.com
WG

**Reem Acra**
245 Seventh Avenue, Suite 6B
New York, NY 10001
212-414-0980
www.reemacra.com
WG, SO

**Regalia Veils**
281 Summer Street, 4th Floor
Boston, MA 02210
617-723-3682
www.fenaroli.com
HP, Veils, Accessories

**Regina B.**
350 Seventh Ave, #2203
New York, NY 10001
212-643-2939
www.reginab.com
HP, Veils, Accessories

**Remy Couture**
200 Fulton Street
Farmingdale, NY 11735
877-736-9274
www.remycouture.com
WG, MOB, SO

**Rena Koh Collections USA**
21000 Boca Rio Road, #A6
Boca Raton, FL 33433
561-470-8894
www.renakohbridal.com
WG, BM

**Renee Romano**
676 N. Dearborn Avenue
Chicago, IL 60610
312-943-0912
www.renee-romano.com
HP, Veils

**Renella De Fina Couture**
345 Millway Avenue, Suite 201
Concord, Ontario, Canada L4K 4T3
905-760-8626
WG

**Reva Mivasagar**
28 Wooster Street
New York, NY 10013
212-334-3860
www.revadesigns.com
WG, SO

**Richard Glasgow**
14 East 38th Street
New York, NY 10016
212- 683-1379
www.glasgowbridal.com
WG, HP, Veils

**Rimini by Shaw**
530 Seventh Avenue, 15th Floor
New York, NY 10018
212-233-1100
WG

**Ristarose Inc., c/o Ginger's**
233 Post Street, Suite M-100
San Francisco, CA 94108
415-781-8559
www.ristarose.com
WG, SO

**Rivini Design, Inc.**
401 Richmond Street W., Studio 216
Toronto, Ontario, Canada M5V 1X3
416-977-1793
www.rivini.com
WG, SO

**Robert Legere**
222 West 37th Street
New York, NY 10018
212-631-0606
www.stevenjs.com/robertlegerebridal
WG, SO

**Romantic Bridals**
363 Lang Boulevard
Grand Island, NY 14072
800-388-5475
WG, BM, SO

**Romona Keveza Collection**
450 Seventh Avenue, Suite 3105
New York, NY 10123
212-273-1113
www.romonakeveza.com
WG

**Ron Lovece**
222 W. 37th Street, 7th Floor
New York, NY 10018
212-868-0895
WG

**Rose Taft**
498 Seventh Avenue, 14th Floor
New York, NY 10018
212-279-8580
www.rosetaft.com
MOB, SO

**Ruby Bridal Design Inc.**
3533 Oak Bend Drive
Arlington, TX 76016
817-446-5096
WG

**Saison Blanche**
145 E. Walnut Avenue
Monrovia, CA 91016
800-358-9281
www.saisonblanche.com
WG

**Salon Shoes**
375 Oyster Point Boulevard, #7
San Francisco, CA 94080
650-588-8677
www.salonshoes.com
Shoes, handbags

**Scala Eveningwear**
1412 Broadway, Suite 1510
New York, NY 10018
212-840-4367
MOB, SO

**Serafina Bridal**
25 West 36th Street, 4th Floor
New York, NY 10018
212-253-2754
BM

**Shannon McLean, Inc./Cose Belle**
7 E. 81st Street, Suite 4
New York, NY 10028
917-838-1547
WG

**Shelley George Design**
209 10th Avenue South, Suite 305
Nashville, TN 37203
888-283-9321
www.shelleygeorge.com
Shoes, Handbags

**Sherry et Cie**
260 W. 35th Street, Suite 300
New York, NY 10001
212-947-6610
www.sherryetcie.com
Accessories

**Silk and Lace Veils**
N110 W16534 Kings Way
Germantown, WI 563022
800-531-2553
HP, Veils

**Siman Tu**
28 West 36th Street
New York, NY 10018
212-904-1218
www.simantu.com
HP, Veils, Accessories

**Simply Charming**
2741 Plaza Del Amo, # 203
Torrance, CA 90503
800-222-9530
www.simplycharming.biz
Accessories

**Siri**
40 D Barneveld Avenue
San Francisco, CA 94124
415-431-8787
www.siriinc.com
WG, BM, SO

**Something New**
13402 Flint Drive
Santa Ana, CA 92705
714-573-9979
HP, Veils

**Songi**
20651 Roscoe Boulevard, #E
Winnetka, CA 91306
818-888-8949
www.songibridal.com
WG

**Special Occasions by Saugus Shoe**
31 Osprey Road
Saugus, MA 01906
800-443-6155
www.bridalshowroom.com/saugusshoe
Shoes, Handbags

**St. Patrick**
15 Main Street
East Rockaway, NY 11518
888-776-6684
www.sanpatrick.com
WG

**St. Pucchi/Avine Perucci**
1511 Main Street
Dallas, TX 75201
800-932-0249
www.stpucchi.com
WG

**Stephanies**
43 River Circle Drive
Logan, UT 84321
435-764-3723
www.stephaniesbridalmillinery.com.au
HP, Veils

**Stephen Yearick**
501 Seventh Avenue, Suite 200
New York, NY 10018
212-221-8188
WG, MOB, SO

**Stuart Weitzman**
50 West 57th Street
New York, NY 10019
212-582-9500
Shoes, Handbags

**Subtle Creature**
111 Arch Street
Philadelphia, PA 19106
215-627-6059
HP, Veils

**Sunny Choi**
117 Peter Street
Toronto, Ontario, Canada M5V 2C9
416-971-9329
www.sunnychoi.com
MOB, SO

**Suzann Designs**
600 W. Van Buren, Suite 904
Chicago, IL 60608
773-205-1733
www.suzanndesigns.com
WG

**Sweetheart Gowns**
808 Cauldwell Avenue
Bronx, NY 10456
800-324-3242
WG, FG

**Sylvain & La Duchesse**
318 West 9th Street, Suite 302
Los Angeles, CA 90015
213-629-2601
WG, SO

**Symphony Bridal**
225 W. 37th Street, 17th Floor
New York, NY 10018
800-992-8345
www.symphonybridal.com
WG

**Symphony Bridal Veils**
225 W. 37th Street, 17th Floor
New York, NY 10018
800-992-8345
www.symphonybridalveils.com
HP, Veils

**Tammy Darling Bridal**
31 South Finley Avenue, Suite 201
Basking Ridge, NJ 07920
908-696-8484
www.tammydarling.com
HP, Veils, Accessories

**Tarina Tarantino Bride**
7211 Santa Monica Boulevard, Suite 200
Hollywood, CA 90046
www.tarinatarantino.com
323-512-8080
HP, Veils, Accessories

**Tatiana Fashions, Inc.**
73 Newbury Street
Boston, MA 02116
617-262-4914
WG

**Thomas Knoell**
80-10 Bell Boulevard
Hollis Hills, NY 11427
866-NY-TIARA
www.thomasknoell.com
HP, Veils

**Tiara Misu**
22 West 32nd Street, 12th Floor
New York, NY 10001
800-517-7222
www.ansoniabridal.com
HP, Veils, Accessories

**Tomasina**
615 Washington Road
Pittsburgh, PA 15228
412-563-7788
www.tomasina.com
WG

**Twinkle-Twinkle, Inc.**
11 Broad Street, Suite 303
Glen Falls, NY 12801
518-745-0894
WG

**Ulla-Maija**
24 West 40th Street
New York, NY 10018
212-768-0707
www.ulla-maija.com
WG

**Unique Imports, Inc.**
2700 Dufferin Street
Unit 18 Toronto, Ontario, Canada M6B 4J3
800-864-7834
www.uniquecouture.com
MOB, SO

**Ursula of Switzerland**
31 Mohawk Avenue
Waterford, NY 12188
800-826-4041
MOB, SO

**Valentina Bridal**
7605 New Utrecht Avenue
Brooklyn, NY 11214
718-331-7500
WG

**Van Herr Bridal**
500 Molino Street, #312
Los Angeles, CA 90013
213-680-3630
www.vanherrbridal.com
WG

**Vanessa Noel Couture, Inc.**
158 E. 68th Street
New York, NY 10021
212-906-0054
www.vanessanoel.com
Shoes

**Vera Wang**
225 W. 39th Street, 9th Floor
New York, NY 10018
800-VEW-VERA
www.verawang.com
WG, BM

**Victoria Royal**
530 Seventh Avenue
New York, NY 10018
212-944-6844
MOB, SO

**Victoria's Bridal Collection**
135 N. Aspan Avenue, # 6
Azusa, CA 91702
626-334-5288
www.victoriascollection.com
WG

**Watters & Watters**
4320 Spring Valley, #108
Dallas, TX 75244
972-404-0143
www.watters.com
WG, BM

**Wearkstatt, LTD.**
260 W. 36th Street, 8th Floor
New York, NY 10018
212-279-3929
www.wearkstattbridal.com
WG

**Windsor Co.**
PO Box 1533
Brick, NJ 08723
732-477-4389
Veils

**Winnie Couture**
3905 Braxton Drive
Houston, TX 77063
713-782-9316
www.winniecouture.com
WG

**Winters and Rain**
208 Bellevue Avenue
Newport, RI 02840
401-848-0868
Veils

**Yolanda Couture**
260 W. 39th Street, 5th Floor
New York, NY 10018
212-398-2010
www.yolandacouture.com
WG

**Youlin**
488 Seventh Avenue, #3G
New York, NY 10018
908-754-5783
www.youlinnewyork.com
WG

**Yumi Katsura**
907 Madison Avenue
New York, NY 10021
212-772-3016
www.yumikatsura.com
WG

**Zoe Ltd.**
112 W. 34th Street, Suite 1621
New York, NY 10120
212-967-2279
FG

## JEWELERS

**A. Jaffe**
37 West 26th Street, 11th Floor
New York, NY 10010
800-223-0553
www.ajaffe.com

**Art Carved/Benchmark**
154 West 14th Street
New York, NY 10011
800-487-4898
www.scottkay.com

**Bianca by Universal**
323 West 8th Street
Los Angeles, CA 90014
800-255-6069
www.biancacollection.com

**Camelot Bridal**
2839 Vauxhall Road
Union, NJ 07083
908-686-0513
www.camelotbridal.com

**Christopher Designs**
42 West 48th Street, 4th Floor
New York, NY 10036
800-955-0970
www.christopherdesigns.com

**Christian Bauer**
1775 West Hibiscus Boulevard, Suite 102
Melbourne, FL 32901
800-228-3724
www.christianbauer.com

**Simon G.**
635 South Hill Street, #703
Los Angeles, CA 90014
800-627-2661
www.simongjewelry.com

**Scott Kay**
780 Palisades Avenue
Teaneck, NJ 07666
800-223-5364

**Tacori**
1736 Gardena Avenue
Glendale, CA 91204
818-863-1536
www.tacori.com

**Varna**
23161 Ventura Boulevard, #203
Woodland Hills, CA 91364
800-993-5900
www.varna.com

**Verragio**
48 West 37th Street, 8th Floor
New York, NY 10018
800-837-7244
www.verragio.com

## STORAGE AND RESTORATION

Once the Big Day has come and gone you may want to store your dress and accessories — even your bouquet — carefully and appropriately. Here are some sources for all the items you'll need to make storing and caring for your wedding wear safe and effective.

### Storage Materials

**The Preservation Station**
www.preservesmart.com

The Preservation Station sells a wedding gown preservation kit that includes everything you need to store your dress properly. They also sell acid and lignin-free tissue papers for wrapping small and large items. Other preservation products are also available through the company's website.

**ArchivalUSA.com**
www.archivalusa.com

ArchivalUSA.com sells museum-quality storage boxes in sizes large enough to accommodate gowns, shoes, and small accessories.

### Gown Restoration Services

**Imperial Gown Restoration**
2814 Merrilee Drive, Suite C
Fairfax, VA 22031
800-WED-GOWN
www.gown.com

**Madame Paulette**
1255 Second Avenue
New York, NY 10022
212-838-6827

### Flower Preservation

**Waterford Past-Thymes**
www.flowerspressed.com

Waterford Past-Thymes presses and preserves flowers. Your wedding flowers are photographed upon arrival so they can be reproduced as closely as possible to the shape of your bouquet. You can also use a sampling of your flowers to surround an invitation or photo or have your flowers artistically arranged "freestyle."

**Flower Preservation, Inc.**
www.flowerpreservation.com

Flower Preservation, Inc., offers high-quality flower preservation services. The company works with each individual bride to preserve her bouquet and offers a wide variety of three-dimensional display options.

# *Index*

# Acknowledgments

Many talented individuals contributed to the development of this book. They are Barry Rosenbloom, Yelena Malinovskaya, Lisa Dickens, Jim Duhe, Michele Hulea, Cybele Eidenschenk, Laurie Brookins, Sara Zick, Maria Zukin and Valerie Passman from *Bridal Guide*. Also thanks to Amy Einhorn, Harvey-Jane Kowal, Sandra Bark and Anna Maria Piluso from Warner Books and Jacqueline Grace from LifeTime Media, Inc. And thanks to Karen Kelly for her editorial contributions and Amy V. Wilson for her creative design solutions.

Thank you also to the many wonderful designers who supplied beautiful images: Anne Barge; Campbell Design; Helen Morley; Ian Stuart; Ines Di Santo; John Russell; Sincerity Bridal; Maggie Sottero; Michelle Roth; Ulla-Maija; Watters & Watters; and Youlin. These designers' beautiful dresses can be found at wedding dress retailers nationwide.